SOVIET VIEWS OF TALMUDIC JUDAISM

*FIVE PAPERS BY YU. A. SOLODUKHO
IN ENGLISH TRANSLATION*

EDITED WITH A COMMENTARY BY

JACOB NEUSNER

Wipf and Stock Publishers
EUGENE, OREGON

Wipf and Stock Publishers
199 West 8th Avenue, Suite 3
Eugene, Oregon 97401

Soviet Views of Talmudic Judaism
Five Papers by Yu. A. Solodukho in English Translation
By Neusner, Jacob
Copyright© January, 1973 by Neusner, Jacob
ISBN: 1-59244-218-8
Publication date: April, 2003
Previously published by E. J. Brill, January, 1973

For my graduate-students at
Brown University

זכרתי לך חסד נעוריך . . . לכתך אחרי במדבר
בארץ לא זרועה

TABLE OF CONTENTS

Foreword IX
List of Abbreviations XIV

I. Slavery in the Hebrew Society of Iraq and Syria in the Second through Fifth Centuries A.D. 1

II. On the Question of the Social Structure of Iraq in the Third to the Fifth Centuries A.D. 10

Commentary
    Jacob Neusner 59

III. The Mazdak Movement and Rebellion of the Hebrew Population of Iraq in the First Half of the Sixth Century A.D. 67

IV. The Persian Administrative-Legal, Socio-Economic, and Everyday Lexicon in the Jewish-Iraqi Literary Monuments of the Sasanian Period 86

V. Concerning Certain Persian Borrowings in the Babylonian *Gemara* 98

Commentary
    Jacob Neusner 104

Index of Talmudic Passages 106
General Index 108

FOREWORD

Devotion to the study of the Babylonian Talmud, a document of law and theology completed in the seventh century A.D. and thereafter the primary and authoritative source of Judaic legal and moral teachings, was one of the distinctive traits of Russian Jewry before 1917. The five papers before us show part of what was accomplished after that time by a Talmudist who also was trained in Soviet historical sciences and Marxist theory. The papers are important for three reasons.

First, they contain important insights and critical perspectives hitherto unavailable to Western scholarship in the history of Judaism in late antiquity.

Second, they underline the importance of introducing into the study of Talmudic and other ancient legal literature a concern for the economic foundations ot the laws.

Third, they provide a glimpse into the mind of a segment of the Soviet Jewish community during its long period of silence, specifically, the segment which evidently attempted to reach an accommodation between the classical Judaic heritage, on the one hand, and the new modes of thought and expression under Soviet Communism, on the other. Solodukho made the effort both to preserve the traditions of Talmudic learning acquired in his youth and to master and make use of the Marxist hermeneutic which came to dominance in his mature years.

Yulii Aronovich (Yudel 'Orelevich) Solodukho was born on June 20, 1877, in Oshmiany, in the former Vilenskaiagubernia, Poland. In 1899 he completed his studies in the famed Yeshiva, or Talmudical academy, of Voloshin. In 1905 he passed the examination for the course of study in the Teachers' Institute of the Riga Educational Region. He specialized in the study of history, and from 1900 to 1915 he collaborated in the work of various journals in Hebrew. From Nov. 1, 1934, to August 15, 1950, he served as a Learned Collaborator of the Oriental Studies Institute of the Academy of Sciences of the U.S.S.R. in Leningrad. Previously, on June 15, 1938, he had defended his dissertation, the theses of which are reproduced below, in the first paper, and this led to the degree of Candidate of Historical Studies. Solodukho died in 1963.

His studies are distinctive and striking because of the sustained effort to introduce into the study of Talmudic religion, law, and history the

Marxist perspectives on class struggle, the role of slavery and entrepreneurship, the development of the middle class, and the like. The first paper, as noted, contains a brief statement of theses. The second, and longest, spells these out in substantial detail, drawing richly upon Talmudic laws, stories, and sayings to substantiate the earlier theses. In the third paper Solodukho applies the theses to the Mazdakite rebellion of the sixth century A.D. The papers tend to a certain repetitiousness and occasional tedium; they have been edited only for style. The editor's critique of Solodukho's fundamental theory and the methods by which he argues and substantiates it are added at the end of the second paper, where Solodukho's approach and methodology are most clearly spelled out and where it is possible therefore to come to a precise and detailed criticism of his results.

I have included two further papers which reveal no significant effort at a Marxist interpretation. The philological studies demonstrate that Solodukho made serious efforts to master the necessary languages and textual traditions for his historical work. He did not come to interpret materials without following the procedures commonplace in Western scholarship. To be sure, one cannot argue he has made an important contribution to the study of Iranian words in the Talmud. Whatever is right in his papers was known before his time; the rest is apt to be wrong—so I am told by an eminent Iranist. For Talmudists, on the other hand, he does bring to the fore the implications of Iranian philological inquiry and makes clear the exegetical importance, in specific contexts, of that study. The final papers therefore allow us to appreciate the methodological concern in Solodukho's work, which, in the time of his activity, certainly cannot have been commonplace, and which even now is hardly routine. If he cannot be called an important Iranist, or even an Iranist at all, he still shows Talmudists what is to be done.

An unpublished manuscript of a full-length book, about 600 pages in length, remains in the archives of the Oriental Studies Institute. It is hoped that, in time to come, a copy of the MS will be made available for translation and study in the West.

The papers were translated by Professor Sam Driver, Brown University, on a grant from The Max Richter Foundation, Inc. The Foundation thereby wishes to express its interest in preserving the scholarly and cultural achievements of the Jewish people under Soviet rule.

The editor further expresses his thanks to Professor E. J. Bickerman, Columbia University and the Jewish Theological Seminary of America, who originally called these and other papers by Soviet Talmudic scholars to his attention and provided photocopies of most of them. Dr. Charles Berlin, Lee M. Friedman Curator of Hebraica at Harvard College Library, kindly supplied copies of other papers. Brown University paid the costs of typing the manuscript and of the index.

The editor does not believe it appropriate to enter into extensive theoretical criticism of the work before us. Apart from commenting on Solodukho's most important paper, he preferred to let the scholar speak without the intrusion of other voices and viewpoints, particularly since Solodukho is no longer available to respond to criticism. Solodukho did his work under circumstances which were, at times, trying, and, always, challenging. He kept alive such Talmudic scholarship as was possible to pursue in his place and period. Clearly, he hoped to effect a synthesis between Talmudism and Marxism and to demonstrate to his learned colleagues the importance of historical and economic inquiry into the religious literature of Judaism. I think he reflects the early hope of Jews that they might preserve and foster their ethnic traditions within the Soviet system. He certainly attempted the most sophisticated, and, historically speaking, authentic part of the task: the enterprise of Jewish learning and of Talmudic study. He is to be taken seriously both as to his scholarly results and as to the larger meaning of his scientific efforts for the history of modern Judaism. That is why the editor wished to accord him the right to be heard for the first time in the West without bickering or competing perspectives. As the work of Solodukho and of other Soviet historians of Jewry and Judaism in late antiquity enters into, and helps shape the development of, the study of that period, time and occasion will suffice for the reconsideration both of specific theses and of general perspectives.

The dedication is to my graduate students at Brown University from the beginning of our program in History of Religions: Judaism in the Department of Religious Studies. In the five years since 1968, these students, risking their scholarly careers in a new and untried program, joined me in the inquiry into the historical problems of studying Talmudic Judaism in late antiquity and in the larger effort to explore the relationships between the enterprise of Jewish learning and of Talmudic study, on the one side, and the cultural and scholarly adventure of American university life, on the other. In our setting we have tried to accomplish what Solodukho did in his, and that is, to see to what degree and in what way one may integrate the classical intellectual heritage of Judaism and the contemporary modes of criticism and interpretation. We do not claim to have achieved entire success, but in rejecting the provinciality, parochialism, and narrow, naive ethnicism of other approaches to Jewish learning, we have confronted the primary dilemma of our subject and have not stood aside from the central task before scholarship on the Jews and Judaism. These students are Dr. David Goodblatt, Haifa University, Professor Robert Goldenberg, Sir George Williams University, Rabbi Shamai Kanter, Professor Gary G. Porton, University of Illinois, Mr. William Scott Green, Mr. Joel Gereboff, Rabbi Baruch M. Bokser, Mr. Charles Primus, and Mr. Jack Lightstone. To them, and to all who come after them, are offered my best efforts.

JACOB NEUSNER

Department of Religious Studies
Brown University
Providence, Rhode Island

15 Shevat 5733
18 January 1973

ABBREVIATIONS

b.	Babylonian Talmud
B.B.	Bava Batra
Ber.	Berakhot
B.M.	Bava Meṣi'a'
B.Q.	Bava Qamma
Dem.	Demai
Eruv.	'Eruvin
Git.	Giṭṭin
Ḥul.	Ḥullin
Ket.	Ketuvot
M.	Mishnah
Meg.	Megillah
M.Q.	Mo'ed Qaṭan
Ned.	Nedarim
Pes.	Pesaḥim
Qid.	Qiddushin
Sanh.	Sanhedrin
Ta.	Ta'anit
y.	Palestinian Talmud
Yev.	Yevamot

CHAPTER ONE

SLAVERY IN THE HEBREW SOCIETY OF IRAQ AND SYRIA IN THE SECOND THROUGH FIFTH CENTURIES A.D.

[The following article, translated by Sam Driver, was first printed in the *Academy of Sciences of the U.S.S.R. Institute of Oriental Studies Bulletin*. It contains the theses of Solodukho's 1938 dissertation. These would be spelled out as his work unfolded.]

I. PROBLEMS OF RESEARCH AND ANALYSIS OF SOURCES

The present work poses the problem of defining the nature [Trans. note: Literally, the "specific gravity"] of slave labor in Hebrew [Jewish] society of Iraq [Babylonia] and Syria [Palestine] II-V cc. A.D., and explaining the real position of slaves in its social and economic structure.

The exploiting classes of the Hebrew population used Talmudic literature for their own interests over many centuries; to this end, they tried to veil the Talmudic literature with religion. Proclaiming the whole Talmudic material sacrosanct and untouchable, they thus preserved it as a charter of class jurisdiction and class attitude. Modern bourgeois researchers obscure the real nature of Talmudic literature and continue along with theologians of all kinds to "preserve" it. For this reason, down to the present time, the Talmudic materials have been used almost not at all in the study of the social problems of Hebrew society in the II-V centuries A.D. Bourgeois historians devoted all their efforts to distort the Talmudic materials concerning slaves in order to create a picture of "ideal" relations between the slaves and their owners.

The period under discussion was for both the Iraqi Hebrews (II-V centuries) and those in Syria (II-IV centuries), a discrete historical period of time, distinctly different from the periods which preceded and followed it. The Second to the Fifth Centuries A.D. were a period of distinct political and economic changes in Iraq and Syria. Because of Rome's suppression of a series of rebellions in Palestine and Syria (I-II century) and their final submission to the power of Byzantium

(IV century), the Hebrew population was ruined and ceased playing any kind of notable role. The rebellion of Asinei and Anilei in Iraq (I century) marked the beginning of the disintegration of slave-owning; the rebellion of Mar-Zutra (VI century) helped bring on the development of feudal relationships.

II. Socio-Economic Structure of Hebrew Society in Iraq and Syria II-V Centuries A.D.

Agriculture was the basic occupation of the Hebrew population of Iraq and Syria at this time. In Iraq, the land was concentrated in the hands of a few members of the upper, hereditary, landholding aristocracy; and also in the hands of tax gatherers and the upper bureaucracy. Along with the aristocrats in Iraq, there were also big landowners who had come out of the milieu of merchants, tradesmen and small landholders. Many of them also engaged in reworking the agricultural raw materials, and carried on considerable trade; this gave to this group of landowners the possibility of acquiring new lands and improving their farms.

With the growth in the number of big landowners, the small landowners were correspondingly impoverished and lost their land. The fields in Iraq needed artificial watering. For the small landowner, the use of the irrigation system was extremely difficult; he was in fact completely dependent on the big landowners. Land and poll taxes came to from one-sixth to one-third of income. Besides these taxes, there were many other duties. The tax burden fell mostly on the small landowners, ruining them utterly. According to Iranian law, "He who pays the land tax has the use of the land." Rich landowners paid the taxes of those who could not pay them and appropriated the lands. The small landowner was often forced to find other means of existence or else to work his former plot of land, not as the owner of it, but as renter or sharecropper. Or, finally, he would be taken on as a hired hand. The estates of the higher aristocracy were farmed basically by slave labor; the farms of the newer landowners were mostly rented out in small parcels to sharecroppers, or were worked by hired hands. The majority of renters and sharecroppers, even with the hardest work, could insure only a very meager existence. Among the hired hands were those who lived on the estate permanently and those who were seasonal and day laborers. The latter group, after work in the fields was done, were often unemployed and without any means of existence.

The developments in land ownership and land use in Syria degraded not only the small landowners, but also some of the big landowners. The Roman Emperors, considered to be the owners of all the land in Palestine, preferred to let the land in huge parcels to the richest renters; these were for the most part members of the landed aristocracy. On the other hand, the severe tax policy of the Roman government in the newly reconquered province completely ruined both the small and middle groups of landholders. As a result, the land was more and more concentrated in the hands of the upper, landed aristocracy. Landholders who only shortly before had been well-off lost their estates and become smaller renters and sharecroppers, or were forced to go into trade or some craft. In regard to the greater amount of land held by the hereditary gentry in Syria, the use of slave labor was more widespread than in Iraq, but even in Syria there was a significant number of renters, sharecroppers and hired men.

Work in trade and crafts had a great significance in the economy of Iraq and especially Syria. Most of the craftsmen could manage to feed themselves by their work. There were, however, some craftsmen who had two or three apprentices, hired men or slaves; there were also small factories where a rather significant number of slaves and hired men worked.

The analysis of the socio-economic structure defines the place of slavery in the economy of this society. Neither the small landowners nor the small craftsmen had the possibility of using slave labor, at any rate, not to any significant degree: "In small landowning and small crafts there was no place for numerous slaves" (Engels).[1] On the other hand, slave labor was widely used to work the lands of the higher aristocracy and the new, emerging class of big landowners.

III. Means of Acquiring Slaves

In the II-V centuries A.D., among the Hebrew population of Iraq and Syria, there were slaves who were both non-Hebrew and Hebrew. Slaves who were non-Hebrew were called Canaanite. This term signifies that the Hebrews originally got their slaves from among the local inhabitants of the land, the Canaanites. There was also a larger number of slaves from other lands. There were slaves from Ethiopia and occasionally slaves from the German tribes. Also attested are the

---

[1] Friedrich Engels, *The Origin of the Family, Private Property and the State*. Moscow, Partizdat (1932), p. 151.

descendants of slaves who had belonged to the Temple and the priesthood during the existence of the Hebrew state. The slave trade in non-Hebrews took place in special "slave markets" located in all cities of some size. To show the slaves to the buyers, the slaves were placed on stone blocks, called "the selling block" or "the buying block." Usually, the sale of slaves was announced beforehand. The price of male and female slaves varied greatly—from one denar to a hundred *minas*. The formula for the bill of sale for a slave has been preserved in the Talmudic literature. The Hebrews also acquired slaves at the big fairs in non-Hebrew cities and in neighboring countries.

Penniless debtors, made slaves by moneylenders, constituted the fundamental mass of slaves who were Hebrews. Small landowners, renters, sharecroppers and tradespeople were forced to borrow in order to pay taxes, buy seed, or feed their families. Non-payment of debts on time meant that the debtors became the slaves of the moneylender. In Iraq, there was a law that "whoever does not pay the poll tax (*karga*) becomes the slave of the man who pays his tax." The big landowners paid for those without means and enslaved them. Those who stole were sold into slavery in order to cover the value of the thing stolen; "useless persons" and those who "conducted themselves improperly," probably the unemployed, were included under the rubric of "useless persons"—the impoverished small landowner or tradesman. It was easy to include among those who "conducted themselves improperly" those persons who tried to struggle against exploitation by the ruling classes, as well as those who broke the religious prescriptions or were charged with atheism. Josephus Flavius also attests that "those who committed a crime against the law" were punished by enslavement. Finally, the impoverished small landowners or tradesmen sometimes sold themselves or members of their family into slavery when there was no other possibility of finding means to live.

IV. THE LEGAL AND SOCIAL POSITION OF THE SLAVES

With regard to law, in the larger part of Talmudic dispositions, a non-Hebrew slave was considered a thing, the full property of the slaveowner. The slave was passed on to the heir, the owner could sell him when and to whom he pleased, could make him over to someone, give him as a gift, and use him as security on a loan or offer him in payment of a debt to a moneylender, who could claim him forcibly before payment. The slaveowner could sell half the slave, keeping the right of property on the other half of his labor. The slave owner could also sell the slave for a time.

Non-Hebrew slaves, according to many Talmudic references, did not have the right to personal ownership and were not legally authorized to make any kind of business deals, even in the name of the owner. A number of Talmudic excerpts, however, speak of the slaves' having their own means: "property to which the owner has no right." There are a number of references which indicate that the slave sometimes carried on the business of his master, traded for him, and even managed his property. There is mention of a master's borrowing from his slave. The references to the slave's lack of right to personal property are a reflection of relations in the earlier period. In time, a new form of exploiting the slaves became widespread: individual slaves were placed on special land plots, and given the means of production. Sometimes the slaveowners made their slaves available for work on the side so that their earnings, entirely or in part, went to the owner. In these cases, the slave had the right to a conditional ownership of property, which in some instances the slaveowner could take back from him. In connection with this new form of exploitation, there was a necessary recognition of the legal rights of the slave.

The spread of this new form of slave exploitation, as well as other relationships between owners and slaves, is reflected in the Talmudic references to the slaveowner's giving the slaves supplies for a certain period of time, and to the question of whether the owner is obliged to feed the slave. Later, the relations between the master and the slave who was placed on separate plots of land or released to work on the side took other forms as well: the slave would return to the owner a certain portion of the harvest from the land he worked or a certain part of the earnings from his work for others. Sometimes, the whole harvest or the whole income from his work for others would remain at the disposal of the slave, but at the same time the slave would have to work for the owner on the owner's fields.

Recognition of any kind of family ties among slaves would have hindered the owners' free disposition of the slaves, selling them when and to whom they chose. For this reason family ties among slaves are denied in the Talmudic literature, both in terms of progenitors and descendants. Similarly, the possibility of legitimate, legal marriage was not recognized between male and female slaves or between them and free persons. These assertions reflect, however, only the relationship of the slaveowners to the slaves, and not the reality of the time. The slaves, as noted above, often had a certain conditional right to property when they were put on separate land plots to farm for themselves; sometimes they received supplies from the master at the beginning of a certain time period. All of this suggests that the slave had a family. The children of slaves of course remained slaves. Children whose mother or father were slaves were accorded the legal status of the mother. Even the children of a slavegirl from an alliance with the master were considered slaves.

Many Talmudic parables and aphorisms show that corporal punishment of the slaves was used. At the same time, we see dispositions concerning the responsibility of the slaveowner for killing his slave, and for administering a punishment which led to the death or crippling of a slave. This is explained by the fact that, with the development of agricultural products and trade artifacts for the market, it became profitable for the owner to expand the production by a more intensive exploitation of the slave, whose capacity for work had to be preserved; this called forth the requirement of "humane treatment" of the slave. Trying to use religion as a means of ideological influence on the slaves, the slaveowners attempted to turn the slaves to Judaism. In certain instances (for example, the border areas), the change of religion to Judaism was required.

The slaves were marked by certain signs showing their condition as slaves and also to whom they belonged. This was done in the first place by tatooed signs. Further, as mark of their station, they wore about their necks or attached to their clothing either bells or a special seal of clay or metal. The slaveowner saw to it that these distinguishing signs were always on the slave and visible; removal or loss was severely punished. Finally, special dress distinguished the slave from freemen. Slaves wore a headcloth, something like a woman's headcloth. There obviously was "slave dress."

A number of dispositions and aphorisms speak of the class antagonism between slave and master and of the struggle against the master. Thus we note, on the one hand, the hatred of slave for master, and on the other, the close friendship among slaves. The mutual interest of the slaves welded them together and united them in the struggle against the master. The slaveowners did not trust their slaves; they feared a destruction of their property by them. It was necessary to free the owner from any responsibility for the losses caused to anyone by the slave, so that the slave could not ruin his master by purposely setting fire to someone else's grain and thus forcing his master to pay the aggrieved party "a hundred *minas* daily." There are many references to runaway slaves. Finally, in certain aphorisms, there are mentions of slave-rebellions. With regard to slaves who were Hebrews, there are many various apparently "humane" dispositions which obscure the real character of the exploitation of this group of slaves. Actually, the position of the Hebrew slaves was not much different from that of the non-Hebrews.

v. The Significance of Slave Labor and Areas of its Use

The Talmudists tried to make acquisition of slaves as easy as possible. In a departure from general prescriptions concerning Sabbath rest and going to non-Hebrew fairs connected with celebrations in honor of local idols, it was permitted to travel to non-Hebrew fairs even on holy days and on the Sabbath if the purpose was buying slaves. A great significance was attached to keeping slaves in the hands of Hebrew slaveowners, and all sorts of obstacles were set up to prevent selling slaves out of the country.

The parallel made between slaves and the land also speaks for the fact that slaves were considered extremely valuable. Thus, for example, when a slave was bought, just as when land was bought, the sale was considered final, even if the buyer had overpaid by twice or more; the amount overpaid did not have to be returned. An especially clear indicator of the great significance of slave labor in Hebrew society of Iraq and Syria of that time is the sharply negative attitude toward manumission. It is noted that "he who frees his slaves ruins himself." If the freeing of a slave took place in any case, then a special certificate of manumission was absolutely required to formalize the matter; it had to be signed by two witnesses or handed over to the slave in the presence of two witnesses. A separate certificate was required for each freed slave.

Slave labor was widely used in various kinds of work. There are accounts of whole villages of slaves being sold, indicating the large size of the properties worked by slaves. The use of slaves in many branches of trades and crafts was widespread. The slaves worked as dyers, tailors, bakers, butchers, barbers, money-changers; they were especially trained for their work. Among the slaves who were craftsmen were highly qualified workers: pearl-drillers, accomplished chefs, among others; they were highly valued. Slave-girls processed wool, threshed grain, baked bread, and so on. Sea trade was very highly developed among the Hebrews of Iraq and Syria; slaves were mostly, or even exclusively, used on the trading ships. Sometimes slaves took direct part in the owner's dealings in trade. Finally, slaves were used for various household tasks and personal service.

There are comparatively little data on the number of slaves in the society, or the number of slaves of individual slaveowners. Indirect references nevertheless suggest a significant number of slaves. In the Hebrew areas of Iraq there were villages entirely populated by slaves, and also manumitted and runaway slaves.

VI. Conclusion

Slavery in Hebrew society of the time under consideration was a significant economic factor. The assertions of bourgeois scholars that slave labor was of little significance do not at all correspond with the reality; nor do the assertions that slaves were used only as personal servants and not for productive work, and that there were no slaves who were Hebrews at the time. One should not conclude from this, however, that slave labor was the basis of production in Hebrew society, the foundation of its economic structure, or that it was a slave-owning society. Besides materials on the great importance of slave labor, the Talmudic literature also contains references indicating doubts as to the efficiency of using slave labor. A number of Talmudic aphorisms characterize the productivity of slave labor in a distinctly negative way: "Ten measures of sleep came down to the earth; the slaves took nine of them and the rest of the world got one." "A slave is not worth the food of his belly." Besides slave labor, the labor of freemen was widely used: renters and sharecroppers in agriculture, hired men in agriculture and the trades. Slave labor, given the condition of greater and greater expansion of production for the market, became less and less profitable because of low productivity. There was a growing tendency to replace slave labor with renters, sharecroppers, and hired labor.

In the Talmudic literature, we note a positive attitude toward labor; a great number of statements praise labor and the man who lives by labor. This attests to the need for a labor force, and the attempt of the exploiting classes to replace slave labor with the labor of other levels of the population. At the same time, many slaves were bound directly to the land: the landowners put the slaves on independent land plots, reserving the right to use part of the harvest, or on the condition that they be given a certain amount of the produce. Or, finally, the slave could keep the entire harvest on the condition that he worked the master's fields at the same time as his own. Such relationships already show the character of the feudal systems of soccage and corvée. Also gradually bound to the land at the time were the renters and sharecroppers who, because of debts, had become completely dependent on the landowner and lost all possibility of leaving the land they rented or sharecropped. Small landowners lost their land and fell into the clutches of the big landowners. While slavery continued and even at times expanded (as under Shapur II, in fourth century Iraq), feudal relationships were already developing in Hebrew society in Iraq in the II-V centuries.

CHAPTER TWO

ON THE QUESTION OF THE SOCIAL STRUCTURE
OF IRAQ IN THE THIRD TO THE FIFTH
CENTURIES A.D.

[This paper, translated by Sam Driver, appeared in *Notes of the Oriental Institute, Moscow*, Vol. 14, 1956, pp. 31-90.]

1. SOURCES

The social history of Sasanian Iraq is scarcely illuminated by Arab and European sources. The most important source is the Babylonian Talmud. Although the data relate only to one particular confessional group of the population of Iraq at that time, the Hebrew, nevertheless the Jewish population did not differ in character of productive activities and social structure from the rest of the population. For this reason the data of the Babylonian Talmud to a certain extent can be used to shed light on the social-economic conditions in Sasanian Iraq and in other more highly developed provinces of Sasanian Iran in general.

The most ancient of the monuments mentioned here is the *Mishnah*, composed between 189 and 219 by the Palestinian, Rabbi Judah the Patriarch. Of a special value as a historical source is the many-volumed Hebrew-Iraqi monument of the time of the Sasanians—the Babylonian *Gemara*, compiled in the course of the third to fifth centuries A.D. in Iraq and edited there at the end of the fifth century. The Babylonian *Gemara* is composed predominantly of short official notes on disputes concerning the discussion of religious prescriptions and legal dispositions in the area of ordinary law, contractual, family and criminal law, practical-legal relationships, as well as the interpretation of Mishnaic legislation for use in the concrete economic and social conditions of Iraq, and notes on the interpretation of various sorts of litigations and disputes. All these materials set forth in the *Gemara* are interspersed with historical, geographical, and astronomical information, philosophical statements and legendary tales. The legal dispositions and propositions are written in Hebrew, the disputes about them in Eastern Aramaic, the living language of Iraq of that time.

The compilers of the Babylonian *Gemara* were striving to work out legal and religious norms. Phenomena of an everyday character and events of everyday life served the compilers of the *Gemara* only as a starting point for laying out legal dispositions. They were the pretext for discussion of corresponding questions of a legal order. They are set forth in an extremely laconic fashion, often in one or two lines. Information relating to one and the same person or event is often scattered through various sections. These materials, especially tales of everyday life, notes of legal processes, and other factual material are most valuable for the researcher.

The overwhelming majority of people who figure in the Babylonian *Gemara* represent a new type of landowner, that is, new in origin, who had moved up out of the milieu of craftsmen and tradespeople and had become rich. Sometimes they were even from the milieu of small landowners. Simultaneously, they continued to be occupied in crafts or trade, or to fulfill state and social duties. In such a social-economic relationship these landowners, in the period under discussion, can be related to the large feudal landholders, which grew up together with the ruling class of not very numerous representatives of the landed gentry. These people were heirs of lands worked for the most part by slaves.

Such affluent landowners were the law-givers of the Babylonian *Gemara*: Abba Arika (d. 247) and Mar Samuel Yarkhinai (165-254) and their main followers: R. Huna (d. 297), R. Nahman b. Jacob (d. 320), R. Hisda (d. 309), R. Joseph b. Hiyya (d. 320), Rabbah (280-352), Huna bar Joshua (d. 410), Abbayye (280-338), R. Papa (d. 375), and others. To this social class also belonged the first editor of the *Gemara*, the head of the Sura Academy, R. Ashi (332-427). (It should be noted in this connection that the dates cited here and below are traditional. They are not exact but most often the lower limits of the possible dating.) The large feudalizing landholders stood for a new, more progressive means of production. They struggled against the gentry, landed by inheritance, who exploited slave labor, and against other large landholders from the milieu of the aristocracy of high rank and of the lease-holders from the government. They therefore represented a more progressive layer of the ruling class. They were, however, especially interested in strengthening the exploitation of the direct producers in agriculture. They sought to institute serfdom and actually to bind to the land the many tenant farmers and sharecroppers, people of their own faith, who belonged to the laboring part of the Hebrew population. To this number also belonged day laborers, day agricultural workers and slaves.

Having taken away the land of the small landholders and turned them, in most instances, into tenants on those plots of land which had earlier belonged to them, the large landholders recognized the need for a new jurisdiction to correspond to new productive relations, in particular in the area of land-owning and land-use. The representatives of these classes of landowners undertook a multi-faceted study of the legal norms in existence up to that time. They made a great effort to work out new norms which better corresponded to the new forms of land-owning and land-use. They therefore undertook a new mutual relation between the proprietors of the appurtenances of the land and the actual owners.

Thus the norm of Talmudic law, a development of biblical civil, criminal and religious legislation, actually was applied to the social-economic conditions of the Sasanian state. Within the limits of this state, the exploiting, upper layer of the Hebrew community supplied a special legal status to the professors of Judaism. They were subject to the temporal head of the community—the exilarch (*resh Galuta*), who occupied an important place in the Sasanian administration. Legal disputes among the professors of Judaism were regulated by their own law. The law which was effective in the courts of the Hebrew religious community was not only applied to existing social-economic conditions, but no longer differed at all from the general norms of the law effective in the Sasanian state.

Having established the class composition of the compilers of the Babylonian *Gemara* and defined their social person, we may say that the material they included in the *Gemara* was subjected to filtration, selection from the point of view of class interest. We may, on the basis of material in the *Gemara*, follow both the dynamics of the process of the birth and the gradual establishment of early-feudal relationships, and also the phenomena accompanying this process: taking the land and enslavement of the small landholders, turning them into tenants, and increasing the exploitation of the direct agricultural producers.

The materials of the Babylonian *Gemara* which form the basis for the present study until now have been little studied and have not undergone an analysis from the position of Marxism-Leninism. They have not been used for solving the corresponding social-economic problems. Bourgeois scholarship carefully works over the teleological and religious materials of the Hebrew monuments, among them the Babylonian *Gemara*, but has given little attention to their social-economic materials. And that is quite understandable. The bourgeois nationalist historians have no reason to concentrate on materials which plainly reveal the class character of the Iraqi-Hebrew society and point up the contradictions of this society: riches and luxury, on one hand, immeasurably heavy labor, material need and half-starved existence, on the other; above all the cruel exploitation of the broad mass of laborers, especially of the direct producers in agriculture. Guided by their class interests, the bourgeois-nationalist historians consciously ignore materials which mercilessly expose their anti-historical conclusions about the special course of development of Hebrew society, the absence of class distinctions within it, the absence, consequently, of premises for class contradictions productive of class struggle.

Materials of a social-economic character are not gathered together anywhere or systematized. A scholarly translation into European languages does not exist. Those translations we do have are inaccurate. For the work at hand the translations have been made anew, directly from the original. They transmit the nuances of separate words and expressions and preserve wherever possible their originality of style. Special attention has been given to uncovering the social essence of both Hebrew and Aramaic terms as well as borrowings from Persian which occur in the monuments in great quantities.

II. THE SOCIAL STRUCTURE OF IRAQ IN THE SASANIAN TIMES
A SHORT SURVEY OF ECONOMICS

The basic economy of Iraq in the third to fifth centuries A.D. was agricultural: grain, vegetables, orchards, and animal husbandry. For this reason in the Hebrew-Iraqi monuments of the early middle ages exclusive attention is given to questions of agriculture and land use. Whole tractates are dedicated to these questions, which are discussed in detail and from many points of view. One finds a mass of concrete facts from the lives of the farmers and the landowners, from the mutual relations between the large and small landowners and the direct producers in agriculture, tenants, hired workers, and slaves. Agriculture flourished in Iraq. The wide area along the middle and lower currents of the Euphrates and the Tigris, today a desert burned by the sun or impassable swamps, then to a significant degree produced rich harvests from pasture lands, vegetable gardens, orchards, and palm groves. The land was thickly settled. Every bit of land good for agriculture was used as pasture, vegetable gardens, or fruit orchards. Rav Judah (218-298) instructed the surveyor Addu: "Do not be careless when you measure, for each little bit of land is good for sowing saffron."[1] Dividing fields between neighbors must be done with great exactness since each bit of land represents significant value. Likewise, R. Hoshaya Rabba (third century) said that "the storehouses of Babylonia are full of grain".[2] Rav (175-247) also affirms that "Babylonia is rich, it gathers abundant harvest without rain".[3]

The fertility of the soil in Iraq was due to the Euphrates and the Tigris and their tributaries, as well as to numerous lakes, and a quite complex system of irrigation. After the spring floods of the Tigris and Euphrates, swamps were left in the low lands. The sun burned the heights. The full flood of the Euphrates and the Tigris began in March–May. In the hottest and driest time of the year, from June–September, the loss of water in the rivers required recourse to artificial watering of the fields. The whole country was covered with a fine network of irrigation and watering devices: various sorts of canals[4] and ditches[5] led the water away from the places which had become swampy; brick or stone dikes, dams, and embankments along the rivers, lakes, and canals preserved the country from floods, protected the fields from flooding, and also contributed to the even distribution of water. The canals and ditches also served to lead the water to the fields, and to numerous wells,[6] pools, and reservoirs for preservation. Constant effort was required to keep the irrigation and watering equipment in order, to clean the rivers, the canals, and the ditches,[7] and to repair in time those water channels which formed in dams and embankments,[8] and often threatened the fields with flood.[9] The Hebrew-Iraqi monuments more than once tell about such water channels and breaks in the dams and embankments.[10]

The landowners had to expend a great deal of work on watering the fields, vegetable gardens, and orchards. It was especially hard for those farmers whose land was located far from rivers and canals. They had to transport or carry water from far away, which took a great deal of time. When certain persons turned to R. Huna (216-297)

---

[1] b. B.M. 107b.
[2] b. Ta. 10a.
[3] *Ibid.*
[4] b. Eruv. 100a, B.M. 107b.
[5] b. Git. 60b, b. B.M. 107b.
[6] b. Ber. 58a, B.Q. 27b, B.B. 91a.
[7] b. B.M. 106b.
[8] b. B.M. 66b.
[9] b. B.B. 41a, Sanh. 7a, Hul. 105a.
[10] b. Eruv. 21a, B.M. 66b, B.B. 41a, etc.

to judge some matter of contention, he would usually announce, "Give me a man to draw water in my place, and I shall solve your dispute."[1] Abayye (280-338) refused Shimi ben Ashi when requested to give Shimi time and to teach him, with the excuse that he lacked free time, since in the daytime he himself was occupied with studies and at night with drawing water for watering his fields.[2]

In the hot time of summer the rivers and the canals of Iraq grew shallow; the level of the water in them dropped sharply; and the shallower canals and ditches fed by them dried up entirely or received an insignificant amount of water, so that there was not enough to water even the fields which lay near the canals and the ditches. This caused constant arguments and disputes among the neighbors, whose fields were situated along the banks of the same river or canal. Arguments concerned taking turns in using water or the right of a landholder to build irrigation equipment. Almost exclusive attention is given to questions of taking turns and using water for watering fields and cleaning rivers and canals from silt. Many disputes and misunderstandings also rose in the case of common ownership of one well or pond. In such instances the owners usually used the water according to an order agreed upon earlier, since there was not enough water for simultaneous usage. Breaking established usage by one of the co-owners called forth a sharp protest on the part of the others.

Hebrew-Iraqi monuments clearly indicate both the nearly exclusive significance of the irrigation and watering system for agriculture in Iraq, and the difficulty of arranging and using it. These same sources bear witness to the fact that the irrigation and watering system of Iraq in the time under consideration was highly developed and had reached perfection, given the level of technical ability of the times. The broad development of the irrigation and watering systems and their excellent condition also allowed for the rise in the quality of agriculture, as noted. Favorable political and economic conditions also contributed.

Handicrafts in Iraq in the third to fifth centuries A.D. reached a significant stage of development. We have information on the development of crafts and the wide-spread craftsmanship from the sources about cities whose population was occupied in craftsmanship, frequently with one particular craft. Numerous data of the sources bear witness to the substantial trade in crafts, and to the existence of craftsmen's corporations and other professional unions, also of in-

[1] b. Ket. 105a.
[2] b. Git. 60b.

dividual organizations for mutual aid, with detailed statutes. The basic branches of craft production were as follows: processing linen, wool and cotton, production of rugs and ready-made clothing, dyeing leather, pottery factories, production of water-proofed felt, mats, twine, pottery vessels, including clay barrels and urns for wine and beer, weaving baskets, serving as tares for vegetables and fruits, wine making and beer brewing, salt preserving and other means of conserving fish, vegetables and fruits, the production of linseed oil and sesame oil, perfumery, making various instruments of production, and polishing and setting precious stones and pearls, and so on. The significance of craft production is shown, in part, by the importance of processing flax and preparation or ready-made clothing; the drop in prices of linen clothing was received as a national catastrophe. In the case of the drop in price of linen clothing to such degree that "the price of ten [dresses] dropped to [the price] of six," that is, they fell in price by forty percent, a general fast was announced "even on the Sabbath,"[1] even though announcing on the Sabbath of any kind of fast at all was strictly forbidden by the Hebrew religion. This shows the production of flax and its further processing were among the basic sources of making a living for the masses of the population. Both flax and the product made from it were exported to other regions of the Sasanian state and to other countries.

The Hebrew-Iraqi literary monuments of the early middle ages contain considerable data about widespread trade in agricultural products and crafts. These data point to the existence of active trade between Iraq and other parts of the Persian state as well as other countries, both by land routes and by the rivers and numerous canals of Iraq, and by the Persian Gulf and the Indian Ocean. As early as the Arsacids, Iran's dominance over the many routes of world trade was established. This dominant position was produced by the establishment, after Alexander of Macedon, of more vigorous relations with India. The beginning of trade, in the second century A.D., between the Near East and China reenforced it. To a greater degree than the Arsacids, the Sasanians exploited this predominance in trade.[2]

The measures taken by the new rulers of the Iranian state created a favorable condition for the development of internal trade as well as transit and contributed to its rapid growth. The increase in trade in its turn contributed to the development of agriculture and craft produc-

---
[1] b. B.B. 91a.
[2] V. V. Bartol'd, *Iran, istoricheskii obzor* (Tashkent, 1926) pp. 20, 21.

tion in reworking agricultural raw materials and called for the growth of productive power. All this in its turn conditioned the further development of trade-monetary relationships. Marx says: "... at the basis of every means of production, trade contributes to the creation of a surplus product, which is destined to go into trade in order to increase the use or treasury of the producers (by this one should understand the owners of the product); consequently it even more gives production the character of production for the sake of trade-value."[1]

The flowering of economic life of the Persian state occurred especially in Iraq, for three reasons. First, as a result of the destruction by Ardashir (226-242) of Mesene, Iraq, which now bordered directly on the Persian Gulf, played a very great role under the Sasanians in trade between the West and East. Second, through Iraq passed the mightiest water arteries of all the Near East, the Euphrates and the Tigris, with their numerous tributaries and canals. Third, Iraq had most fertile soil and a wide network of irrigation and watering arrangements, which the Sasanians developed. The economic rise and growth of productive forces called forth great changes in the character of the productive relationships in all the areas of the economic life of Iraq. They changed the nature of the social structure of the country. This is clearly seen in the area of agriculture, at the time under consideration the basic occupation of the population of Iraq and the basic economy of the country.

III. The Hereditary Gentry and the Feudal Landowners

As was noted above, the monuments of Hebrew-Aramaic literature serve as a valuable source for research into the social-economic structure of Iraq and other economically developed provinces of Sasanian Iran. These sources are especially important for the study of the system of land relationships. While they illuminate directly only the relationships within the framework of the Judaic community in Iraq, the sources may also give some idea about agrarian relationships in the province as a whole.

Up to the period under discussion, the direct producers in the agrarian economy of Iraq were primarily free farmers, individually working plots of land which belonged either to them personally or

---

[1] K. Marx and F. Engels, *Soch.*, Vol XIX, Chap. 1, p. 253.

to the village community. Beside small landholdings of the direct producers and the communal use of land was large landownership. Large landowners were not very numerous. They represented hereditary landed gentry of the ranking aristocracy, and leasers of state taxes. Their lands, as noted above, were worked in the main by slaves. Both the exilarchs, the hereditary administrators of the Sasanians among the Hebrew population, and the members of their family owned large landed properties. Evidence of the immense extent of landholdings of members of the families of the exilarchs is, for example, the tale about "the son of [the exilarch] Mar Samuel [the first half of the fourth century A.D.] who ordered [before his death] to give on a yearly basis 13,000 zuz^1 to Rava (d. 352) from the income [from his holdings, located in the extreme south of Iraq near the river of Paniia]."[2] R. Naḥman (third century), the son-in-law of the exilarch or one of his close relatives, was likewise rich; his wife, in a fit of anger, "went into the wine house [storehouse for wines] and broke 400 vessels of wine."[3] Many other members of the families of the exilarch were equally rich. No less immense were also the landholdings of other noble clans. Thus the holdings of a certain Nitzoi (NYṢW'Y) even exceeded in size the holdings of the exilarchs.[4] Concerning the huge holdings of the tax farmers we have a story-legend about the riches of R. Huna b. Ḥiyya (third century), a tax farmer, who was able to prepare for four hundred learned men who were coming to visit him "four hundred golden arm chairs."[5]

At the beginning of the second century, alongside the great noble landholders who used slave labor on a wide scale and who were connected with the government administration, a new group of landowners appeared. These men had come out of the milieu of merchants, craftsmen, and sometimes even the small landholders. They also owned significant lands and great estates. One can judge the size of such estates from a tale about Abba bar Abba (second to third centuries) and his son Mar Samuel, representatives of that group of landholders indicated here. Abba bar Abba would sell his agricultural products from his holdings immediately after the gathering of the harvest, wishing to forestall by this means the possibility of a

---

[1] A *zuz* is the same as a *denar*, a silver coin of 3.6 grams, worth a Roman *denarius*.
[2] b. Ned. 55a.
[3] b. Ber. 51b.
[4] b. Eruv. 59a.
[5] b. Ber. 31a.

rise in prices for food. His son, Mar Samuel, did not do that until the prices on corresponding produce began to rise. He then tried to lower the prices and to forestall a further rise.[1] To influence prices in the markets of such a large city as Nehardea, where Abba bar Abba and his son, Mar Samuel, lived, it would have been necessary to have at their disposal a significant quantity of such produce and to own immense land. Moreover the sources, which quite frequently note the riches of persons mentioned, never point out Abba bar Abba or his son, Mar Samuel. Evidently, certain representatives of this group of landholders had still larger landholdings than theirs. Other tales are no less indicative of the size of the landholdings of the landowners of the new type. R. Huna (216-297) once had four hundred vessels of wine go sour.[2] These four hundred vessels of wine, judging by the context, made up only a part of the harvest of his vineyards, received by him in the same year from one of his numerous sharecroppers. Geniva (third century) bequeathed to Abina four hundred *zuz* from the income of his vineyards, located near the river Paniia in the south of Iraq.[3]

Many of these large feudal landholders also reworked agricultural raw material into cloth, rugs and baskets, beer, wine, and so on. Some at the same time carried on important trade in agricultural produce, in the artifacts of craftsmen, and also in various trade-goods imported from countries far and near. Along the rivers and the numerous canals, which cut through the entire country and which united the Euphrates with the Tigris, they sent grain and cereals, wines and various sorts of beer, into the less fertile places inside the country and into various regions of Iran; they also made use of land or sea routes through the Persian Gulf and the Indian Ocean into other countries. Thus for example the landholder Abba Arika [= Rav] (d. 247) owned an immense vegetable farm[4] and got rich from beer brewing. Also rich in brewing were the landholders R. Ḥisda[5] (217-309) and R. Papa[6] (fourth century). R. Huna, who in his youth was a small landholder,[7] got rich in later life thanks to manufacturing and trading in wine.[8]

---

[1] b. B.B. 90b.
[2] b. Ber. 5a.
[3] b. Git. 65b.
[4] b. M.Q. 12b, Qid. 33a, B.B. 54a.
[5] b. Pes. 107a.
[6] b. Meg. 28a.
[7] b. Ket. 105a.
[8] b. Meg. 28a.

R. Huna sold wine which went sour for the price of good wine, since vinegar at that time was expensive.¹ The landowner R. Huna ben Joshua (d. 410) traded in sesame-seed-oil, which he bought in areas located along both banks of the King's Canal (Nehar Malka), and transported it by that same canal.² Landholder Abba bar Abba mentioned above traded in silk.³ In the city of Nisibis he offered his silk as credit to Judah ben Bathyra (second century).⁴

Income from crafts and trade gave this group of landholders the possibility of acquiring new lands. The lands which they acquired in their turn became a real source of significant income, contributing to further wealth. The amount of land in Iraq was limited; land therefore represented a thing of great value. Every plot of land which was good for agriculture was put to use. Even the banks of the rivers, canals, and ditches⁵ were taken by force. Usually four cubits on each side were left free for the needs of the barge haulers. The banks of the canals and rivers were considered common property, and the banks of ditches belonged to the owners of the nearest fields. Later on, the state itself began to sell strips of free land, located along the banks of the rivers and canals, and it was noted in the bill of sale that to the buyer of such land belongs also the part which lay along the river up to a certain place in its width. The sources point out: "Now the Persians [representatives of the Persian government] write [in the bills of sale]: 'I have acquired for myself to the depth of a horse's neck in water.'"⁶ That is, together with the land, the buyer had acquired also that part of the river lying next to the land up to that point in its width where water would reach the neck of a horse. The paucity of available land and its high price led in the third century in Iraq even to the prohibition of raising of smaller domesticated animals, whose keep requires significant free plots of land for pasturage. To Abba Arika is attributed the following: "We have made Babylonia [Iraq] like Palestine [we have equated Iraq with Palestine] in regards to smaller domestic animals."⁷ That is, raising them was forbidden in Iraq, as it had been forbidden before that time in Palestine. The Palestinians' rule was that "smaller domesticated animals are not

---

¹ b. Ber. 5b.
² b. Git. 73a.
³ b. B.Q. 117b, Midrash Shemuel 10.
⁴ Midrash Shemuel 10.
⁵ b. B.M. 108a.
⁶ b. B.M. 107b.
⁷ b. B.M. 108a.

raised in Palestine, but are raised in Syria (outside of Palestine, where no insufficiency of free land for pasturage was felt) and in the deserts of Palestine,[1] which were not good for grain raising or gardens. Iraq originally had no necessity to limit raising smaller domesticated animals; there had been sufficient land for animal husbandry, which had played originally a great role in the rural economy of Iraq, especially on the estates of large landholders. But the considerable development of agriculture led as early as the second century to acute shortage of land. For that reason, in the beginning of the third century, when Abba [Rav] came from Palestine to Babylonia,[2] a similar rule was adopted in Iraq forbidding the raising of smaller domesticated animals.

It is not surprising that there was a very strong competition among those who desired to acquire land; everyone tried to outdo the other in purchasing a plot of land which had come on the market. R. Papa advised: "Hurry to buy land."[3] If land comes up for sale, one must not be slow in closing the deal, since it will be acquired by someone else among the many contenders for it. The rush for land led often to sharp conflicts, altercations and various complaints. If one would buy a plot of land, another might expropriate it to himself by one or another means,[4] and, in general, acquire the plots of land of others by deception or simply by force.[5] In the sources are preserved disputes concerning to whom one or another plot of land belonged.[6]

In order to stop competition during the buying and selling of lands a law was adopted in Iraq concerning the "neighboring owner" (BR MṢR') according to which, in case of the sale of a plot of land, of a vegetable garden or of an orchard, the man who owned lands adjacent to the plot of land being sold had the predominant right to acquire them, that is, the man who was the nearest neighbor of the seller of the real estate.[7] If anyone should acquire land by getting around this law or by breaking it, the sale had to be declared null. The land sold had to be transferred to the buyer who was the neighboring landholder.[8] But this disposition was used widely only by the large feudal landholders, in order not to permit the small landholders

---

[1] M. B.Q. 7:7, M. Dem. 11:5, b. B.Q. 79b.
[2] b. B.Q. 80a.
[3] b. Yev. 63a.
[4] b. B.B. 54b.
[5] b. B.B. 40b, 168b.
[6] b. B.B. 30a-b, 32a-b, 33b.
[7] b. B.M. 108a-b.
[8] b. B.M. 108a-b, 33b.

to acquire new lands. The law had no practical significance in diminishing competition. Many exceptions to the general law, made to the advantage of large landholders, left loopholes for the contenders for the land and gave them the possibility of ignoring it completely. It is sufficient to cite here several exceptions to the general disposition, in order to see its true character and consequences. "If the money of one man [not the neighboring buyer] is good [current], and the money of another [the neighboring buyer] is of full weight [but not in good demand]—there is no law concerning the neighboring buyer."[1] The seller of the land had the right to state what he wanted, namely money that was in good demand. Further, "if the neighboring buyer says: 'I shall go and I shall try to bring the money,'—they do not wait for him; [and it] he should say: 'I shall go and I shall bring the money'—(then) they see: If he is a rich man who will go and bring the money, they wait for him, and if not, they do not wait for him."[2] If there are various neighbors on various sides of the land to be sold and one of them preceded the other neighboring landholders and bought the plot of land, then the deal was considered binding.[3] In all such instances, when one of the buyers could propose to the seller of the land a more profitable condition than others, the law about the "neighboring owner" lost its force. Obviously, the richer contender for the land could offer the seller more profitable conditions; he could always get the money faster, he always had money on hand, and therefore it was not necessary to wait; and if it was necessary to wait, then people waited for him, since they were sure that he would return at the agreed time with the necessary money. The law of the "neighboring owner" also lost its force when anyone wanted to sell all his lands in various places to a single buyer.[4] It goes without saying that buying many plots of land at once could be done only by a large landholder. If a small landholder wanted to acquire one of the plots of land being sold, such a purchaser could not, in such circumstances, make use of his right of the "neighboring owner."

Furthermore, this law did not apply if a lender wanted to acquire the land, if the lender had accepted the land as a security for assuring repayment of a debt.[5] Making use of this exception to the general law

---

[1] b. B.M. 108b.
[2] b. B.M. 108a-b.
[3] *Ibid.*
[4] b. B.M. 108a-b.
[5] *Ibid.*

of the neighboring owner, the larger landholder could always give a loan to the person planning to sell his lands, with the land as security. Afterwards he could acquire the land and thus circumvent the law about the "neighboring owner."

IV. Land-Taking and the Enslavement of the Small Landholders

The rush of the hereditary nobility and the large feudal landholders for land had destructive consequences for small landholders. This led on the one hand to the destitution and loss of land of the small landholders, and on the other to their gradual enslavement by gentry and by large landholders of the new type and finally to their complete serfdom. [Translator's Note: This is serfdom in the Russian sense, which means that the serf was tied to the land and sold with the land.]

The land of the small landholders could not be expanded. The hereditary nobility and the large feudal landlords did not permit the small landholders to obtain any new land holdings at all. Besides, the small landholders could not do so because of their lack of the necessary material resources. It became more and more difficult for them to preserve even the small land plots which they did have, to resist the pressure of powerful neighbors, the money-lenders and tax-farmers, all striving to grab off their land and to enslave them.

R. Eleazer (third century) states: "Land is not given (to anyone)—except to the strong (B'LY ZRW'WT),"[1] that is to the all-powerful landholders. Only they could be considered masters of their immense landholdings. Land only nominally belonged to the small landholders on the other hand; the actual owners were feudal landholders of the new type, to whom the former were in complete slavery, and who at any time could take their land from them and make it their own.

The small landowners in Iraq had insignificant plots of land. Their worth was usually equal to fifty, and the largest of them to one hundred, *zuz*.[2] Each time the plots of land of the small landholders are mentioned, their value is consistantly indicated by just such a sum. Thus it is said: "One man owed 100 *zuz*, and he died, and he left a field worth 50 *zuz*. A money-lender came and took it [the field]."[3] "One man who owed one hundred *zuz* had two small plots of land.

---
[1] b. Sanh. 58b.
[2] b. Ket. 91b, Yev. 63a.
[3] b. Ket. 91b.

One he had bought for fifty *zuz* and the other for fifty. A moneylender came and took one of them; again he came and took the other."[1] We thus see that ordinary measurements of the plots of landowners had the value of fifty *zuz*. Furthermore, even those small plots of land which the small landowners did have at their disposal were often far-flung in various places and divided by strips of land. The field of the small landholder, limited in size, was sometimes merely a series of scattered, still smaller land plots; this complicated working them and served as a reason for the loss of much extra time and labor: "Man does not live a little bit here, a little bit there, but in regard to his sowing, it often happens that a man sows here a little bit, there a little bit."[2] Not infrequently two or several small landholders would together work a single plot of land so small in its size that its division among them was entirely impossible. The sources cite a detailed discussion of the question of how, given such minimal sizes, the co-owner can force his companion to make a division of the real estate, which had up to that time been in their common use.

Since the idea of a minimal land plot, useful for raising grain or vegetables, is not the same everywhere, but depends on the local conditions—the fertility of the soil, the intensiveness of working the land, and so on—the question is posed: "How is it in Babylonia [Iraq]?"[3] That is, at what size of the field may a co-owner require its division in Iraq? R. Joseph (d. ca. 322) answered: "At a size where it takes one day to plow it."[4] The meaning is that after division each of the companions has to receive a land-plot, the plowing of which will take one working day. In the division of an orchard it was required, according to the statement of Abba bar Abba (second to the third centuries), that after the division there be three *qavs* for each of the companions.[5] A lot less than three *qavs* in size cannot be used for an orchard. In the opinion of Rava on dividing a vineyard in Iraq, it was required that each should receive "three rows and twelve grape vines in each row—as much as a man can work in a day."[6]

---

[1] *Ibid.*
[2] b. B.M. 118a.
[3] b. B.B. 12a.
[4] *Ibid.*
[5] b. B.B. 12a *Qab* is a measure for granular and liquid measure, equal to four *logs*. A log = 549.4 cubic cm.; consequently, a *qab* = 2197.6 cubic cm., or 2.2 litres. Measures of space were determined by the amount of grain sown on that space. Thus *bet qab* is a plot on which a *qab* of grain has been sown.
[6] b. B.B. 12a.

The difficult position of the small landholders was caused not only by the insignificance of their land plots, but also by the weight of taxes. The land tax, as will be shown in detail later, took from the landholder from one-third to one-half of his income.[1] However, as a result of malfeasance and extortion of the civil servants, engaged in gathering taxes, and the farmers, the over-all sum of the taxes grew even greater.[2] There existed also poll taxes and a whole series of duties. The larger landholders could in one or another way get rid of the claims of the civil servants and the tax-farmers, transferring all the weight of the land taxes and other duties to the small landholders. The pressure of taxes weighed for the most part on the small landholders and finally destroyed them.

Land-tax was so burdensome for the small landholder that he was sometimes made to give up his land for rent equal only to the price of paying off the land tax, not requiring of the lessee any additional payment in rent.[3] When he could not find a lessee even on such conditions, there was often nothing left for him to do except for him to throw up his lands to the whim of fate and to take flight from the cruel persecutions awaiting him, even to the point of being sold into slavery to tax-gatherers and the tax-farmers.[4] The land and appurtenances of those who took flight were sold under the hammer by the government civil servants charged with gathering taxes,[5] the tax-farmers, and the local court of judicature, without observing any formalities usually required in similar sale.[6] Or a farmer simply gave himself to anyone who would agree to pay up the taxes accrued on his land. Such a sale of land by the poor payers of the land tax then was in Iraq quite ordinary. The actual law, protecting the interests of the ruling class, did not see anything prejudicial in the act of those who used such opportunities in order to acquire for themselves other people's lands, for "the law of the state is the law."[7]

In order to pay taxes, to buy seed for sowing, and repair the equipment of production which was in disrepair, and not infrequently even to feed the family until the new harvest, the small landholders

---

[1] Nöldeke, *Tabari*, p. 241, n. 1.
[2] b. B.Q. 113a, b. Sanh. 25b.
[3] b. Ned. 46b.
[4] b. B.M. 33b.
[5] b. B.B. 55a.
[6] b. B.M. 108b.
[7] b. Git. 10b, Ned. 28a, B.Q. 113a, B.B. 45b, 55a.

were forced to have recourse to loans against the future harvest[1] or to a forehand sale of the future harvest at any extremely low price.[2] The practices of taking loans against the future harvest and the advance sale of the harvest were very widespread in Iraq in the third to the fifth centuries. One can judge that this is so since in the legal sources of that time much attention is devoted to questions connected with loans and advance sales against the coming harvest. Various sorts of loans and conclusions of sales were discussed in detail.

Loans with the land plots as security were given out usually for some period of time agreed upon when the loan was received, up to ten years and sometimes more.[3] During the course of the whole agreed time, the man who had given his land as security did not, in many parts of Iraq, have the right to pay off the loan and buy himself out.[4] But even if the length of the loan was not affixed earlier, for the course of a year the indebted person could not pay up and buy back the land which he had given as security. R. Ashi (d. 427) notes on the part of the "elders" of the city of Mata Meḥasia that the "usual mortgage is a year."[5] If the length of the period of the loan had not been agreed upon earlier, then, until the course of a year from the day of the mortgage, the indebted person did not have the right, having paid this debt, to require the mortgaged land to be returned. For the whole time of the mortgage the money-lender had the use of the land mortgaged to him and received all the income from it. Most often the money-lender had the use of the mortgaged land "without deduction" (BL' NKYYT').[6] That is, the income received from the mortgaged land was not deducted from the sum of the debts. The debt was not lessened thereby. But even in those areas where it was accepted to apply this income against the debt, the income was not counted in full, but only in part, and not from the very beginning, but only after several years had gone by. In such areas, when land was mortgaged, the parties agreed about how many years the money-lender would use the product of the fields free, and after how many years he would have to count the income from the field against the amount of the debt. In the mortgage document it would say, for example, "To five years I will eat it without any deduction; after that and thence forth

---

[1] b. B.M. 72b.
[2] b. B.M. 73a-b.
[3] b. B.M. 67b, 109b.
[4] b. B.M. 67b.
[5] b. B.M. 67b, 68a.
[6] b. B.M. 67b.

I will accredit to you all the fruits."¹ The city of Sura in this regard was an exception: there the income from mortgaged land in part was deducted from the very beginning against the amount of the debt, and in the mortgage it was said, "After the passing of so many years the land will go back to the man who mortgaged it without money,"² that is, without any redemption.

After receiving his lands from the small landholder as security for money loaned to him, the money-lender frequently rented these lands immediately to their original owner. In the city of Naresh this was so common and general a practice, that there was a fixed formula for the corresponding agreement: "I have mortgaged such a land of mine to so-and-so, and afterwards I rented it back from him."³ This formula for the agreement, however, has seemed to certain students of law to oversimplify; it hides nothing and does not mask the exploitation of those indebted by the money-lenders. The income received by the moneylenders from their peculiar "sharecroppers" clearly had, in such a formulation, the character of usurious percentages. Therefore the students of law introduced, instead of the formula indicated, a more "perfect" one, which gave such transactions the character of buying and selling, but in essence changing nothing: "He has mortgaged such land of his to so-and-so, and he bought it from him [the indebted person], he held it for a certain time, and afterwards rented it out."⁴

Mortgaging lands often led even to their final loss by their owners and to the transfer of the land plots to the full possession of the money-lenders. Exerting pressure on the people indebted to them, the money-lenders could force them to extend the length of the mortgage, and then require selling the mortgaged lands after the time of the mortgage had run out, or even before that time. In order to force the indebted person into sale of the mortgaged lands, the money-lenders would also use the law of superannuation (ḤZQH).⁵ According to this law, if anyone who had the use of land or other real estate for the course of three years should announce that this land or real estate is

---

¹ b. B.M. 67b.
² b. B.M. 67b, B.B. 38a.
³ b. B.M. 68a.
⁴ b. B.M. 68a.
⁵ Ḥazaqah (ḤZQH) means literally, "to fasten," "to consolidate," and was used in the sources as a technical term in jurisprudence. In the given instance it means the superannuation of ownership *(usucario)* the acquisition of the right of ownership of property by means of using it for a certain period of time, namely, three years.

bought by him, his right of property to it was recognized without any witnesses and without showing the bill of sale, on the basis of only this law of superannuation.[1] The following tale illustrates the matter: "A certain man mortgaged his orchard to his neighbor for three years. After that, when the loan-giver had used its fruits for three years of superannuation, he said to the indebted one, 'If you will sell it to me, good, and if not, I shall hide the agreement about the mortgage, and I shall say it is bought by me.'"[2] Similar misuses of the law of superannuation took place quite frequently.[3] Another means for exerting pressure on the debtor was the condition entered into the mortgage contract that if the debtor should wish to sell his mortgaged lands, he has to sell them exclusively to the lender for that sum which was loaned him or for a price which would be fixed at the time of sale.

Small landholders completely depended on the gentry and large landholders through loans and mortgage of their lands. This dependence also arose in connection with the necessity of building various types of irrigation equipment, keeping it in working order, cleaning it systematically, and making periodic repairs. The irrigation equipment of large size was taken care of by the central government. It also was concerned with keeping that equipment in working order. The construction of less significant equipment of a local character and also repairing and renewing it fell to the obligation of the large landholders. All this was far beyond the means of the small landholders. This local irrigation equipment served, in the hands of the large landholders, as a means of bringing the small landholders under subjection to them, in the same fashion as the irrigation system in general was in the East a source of despotic power. The large landholders could at any moment deprive the small landholders of water. All they had to do was deepen the bottom of a canal in some place or other, or deepen a river which flowed through their immense estates, or hold up by some means the normal flow of the canal or the river. The fields of the small landholders taking water from that canal or river would be deprived of water, and their owners would be given over to hunger and to complete ruin.

The transfer of lands of the small landholders into the hands of the hereditary gentry and the large landholders of the new type also was helped in no small way by the law, mentioned above, concerning the

---

[1] b. B.B. 29a.
[2] b. B.B. 40b.
[3] b. B.B. 33a, 38a.

"neighboring owner." According to that law the preeminent right to acquisition of land being sold belonged to the neighbor of the seller and to him who owned those plots of land bordering on the lands for sale. In view of the immense size of the estates of the large and affluent landholders, any plot of land for sale always turned out to border their holdings. This fact already predecided the question of who would acquire this plot.

The fate of the majority of the small landholders deprived of their lands was the same. They were turned into sharecroppers. Having lost the right of property to the land, they often continued to work it, but now as renters. Continuing to work the lands as they had up to this time, they were forced now to give up the lion's share of the harvest and other income from their own former properties to the person to whom the property right has passed. The estates of the old slave-owning gentry, of the higher ranking aristocracy, and of the large tax-farmers were worked by slaves. The fields, vegetable gardens, and orchards of the new strata of the class of landowners were predominently rented, in small plots, to small landowners who had lost their lands, and, in the majority of cases, their former owners, who were now bound to the land.

V. MAKING TENANT FARMERS INTO SERFS

Renting lands took various forms and in the sources appears under different names, independently of the object being rented and of the means by which the land rent was paid. First, in one form of rent, which was very widespread, the amount of land-rent did not depend on the size of the harvest, that is on the income of the renter. Moreover, if the land rent was paid in the form of a fixed amount of money, then the use of the lands belonging to another was called *sekhirut* (hire). If the land rent was paid in the form of a fixed quantity of produce, independent of the size of the harvest, then renting to another for temporary use of the land was called *khakirut* (rent).[1]

Independent of the terms of the rent agreement concluded with the landholder, the renter *(khōker)* paid the land rent either in the fruits from his rented land or by means of some other agricultural produce. We have stories about a man who "rented a vineyard for ten barrels

---

[1] The sources themselves point to this difference between *sekhirut* and *khakirut* in this way: "What [is the difference] between *sokher* and *khoker*? *Sokher* is for money; *khoker* is for produce." Tos. Dem. 6:15-16. [Ed.: ḤKR.]

of wine,"[1] and another who rented land for the sowing of clover for several *kors* of barley. The renter did not have the right to break the corresponding conditions of the contract. Thus, for example, the renter, having agreed with the landholder to pay his land-rent in wheat from the rented field, not only did not have the right to pay the rent in some other grain, but could not even pay it with purchased wheat, even when the purchased wheat was in its quality better than the wheat from the rented field. The landholder could say: "I want the wheat from my own field."[2]

The renter *(khōker)* was in this way deprived of the right of sowing the field rented by him with grain according to his personal desire. He was obliged to submit to the will of the landowner and to work those crops which were profitable for the landowner and which had already been provided for by the rent contract. The renter *(sōkher)* was also bound to the conditions of the contract or the norms of local law—"by the custom of the region" *(Minhag hamedina)*. He did not have the right to sow the rented field with grain of his own choice because various grains to various degrees wear out the soil.[3] It was considered, for example, that barley exhausted the soil less than wheat, that wheat exhausted the soil less than sesame, and that flax exhausted the soil more than all other grains.[4]

A form of renting out land which was even more widespread was sharecropping, under which the person who received lands for temporary use had to pay the owner a fixed portion of the harvest received by him: from one-third to one-quarter. Sharecropping also was of two kinds, and, in correspondence with the conditions agreed upon, it was called *'arisut* or *qabblanut*. The sharecropper *('aris)* was smaller and more dependent on the landowner than the sharecropper *(qabbelan)*. The sharecropper *('aris)* owned the tools of production only in part; together with the land, the landowner would give him also certain tools of production: a hoe, spade or shovel, to aid in fertilizing the land with manure, a ladle for artificial watering and a leather bag, probably for carrying or transporting water from the river, the canal, or the well onto the field.[5] The conditions of sharecropping *(qabbelanut)*

---

[1] b. B.M. 106a.
[2] b. B.M. 105a. It is possible that this formula was in its own way a reflection of that process of turning the small producer into a serf, the question under discussion here.
[3] M. B.M. 9:8.
[4] M. B.M. 9:9, Tos. B.M. 9:31.
[5] b. B.M. 103b.

were quite different. On the *qabbelan* fell all of the responsibility for the lands which they had taken as sharecroppers: the construction of the more significant irrigation equipment[1] [the minor irrigation work not connected with significant monetary expenses had to be done by the sharecropper ('aris)], care of the tools of production and of the seeds, paying taxes and so on. For this reason the part of the harvest which the sharecropper *(qabbelan)* had to give the landowner was incomparably less than that part which the sharecropper *('aris)* was obliged to give. While the latter had to give the landowner from one-third to three-quarters[2] of all of his harvest, the sharecropper *(qabbelan)* gave, in all, only from one-quarter to one-third or one-half. Renting land for sharecropping to the sharecropper *(qabbelan)* for only one-third profit to the landholder, or even for only one-quarter, took place when there was a need for a great deal of preparatory work and the loss of significant resources in order to turn a land plot which had not been worked earlier into arable land suitable for sowing.

    This sharecropper *('aris)* was in certain areas of Iraq not even able to insure himself independently of having grain for sowing; the landowner gave him the grain. In the sources it says that in different areas, different practices existed in this regard. In some places the seeds were given to the sharecropper *('aris)* by the landholder; in other places the sharecropper supplied the seeds. In actuality the landowner provided the sharecropper with seeds even in areas of the better sort, since in practice the sharecropper did not have the means of acquiring the seed for sowing. The seeds were bought against his account, and the funds spent on their purchase were charged against the debt of the sharecropper to the landholder. On reaping the harvest, the sum spent on buying the seed, undoubtedly with an addition of corresponding interest, was accounted to the landowner out of the part of the harvest which belonged to the sharecropper. The responsibility of the sharecropper to provide seeds was, in the hands of the landowner, merely another means of exerting pressure on the sharecropper, and gave the landowner, if he so wished, an excuse for breaking the contract and getting rid of the sharecropper. The following disposition attests to this: "In a place ... where the sharecropper gives seeds, whether he has already gone on to the land to be sharecropped or not, as long as he has not given the seed, the landholder can get rid of

---

[1] Minor irrigation work, not connected with significant monetary outlays, had to be done by the sharecropper-*'aris*.
[2] b. Git. 74b, B.M. 109b, 110a.

him; ... in a place where the owner of the land gives the seeds ... if the sharecropper has entered the land, the landholder cannot get rid of him."[1] Referring to the fact that the sharecropper did not have seed in time, the landholder could legally break the contract agreed upon by him and the sharecropper and could chase him from the rented land.

The landholder also paid the taxes on the land rented out for the sharecropper (*'aris*). Concerning this there is the statement of Rava (d. 352)," *'Aris* takes his portion (part)"[2] from the threshing floor *whole*,—that is, without any deductions for the taxes paid on the land rented by him. The landholder does not have the right to deduct anything from the part of the harvest belonging to the sharecropper for the paying of taxes, since taxes on the lands rented to the sharecropper have to be paid entirely on his part, from his portion of the harvest.

Besides a large part of the harvest, the landowners kept all the straw, which was highly valued in Iraq and necessary for the sharecropper to feed his domestic animals and for heating. R. Joseph said, "In Babylonia it is accepted practice not to give the straw to the sharecropper ... and if there is a man [landholder] who gives [a part of the straw to the sharecropper], that is charity and his example is not followed."[3] Such a "generous or charitable" deed on the part of the landowner with regard to his sharecropper does not serve as proof of the existence in a given region of a custom of giving to the sharecropper a part of the straw; it is not a precedent by which others were obliged to be guided in dividing up the harvest with their sharecroppers.

The sharecropper was obliged to deliver the part of the harvest belonging to the landholder in prepared condition, a fully worked product: the harvest of the field had to be threshed, winnowed, and swept into a pile of grain; the harvest from the vineyards had to be in the form of wine[4] and so on. We have the formula of a contract preserved in sources going back to the third century A.D., as follows: "I shall go and till the land, sow, reap, bind into sheaves, winnow, and I shall place the pile before you; and you will come and take half, and I will take half for my labor and for the use of my hands."[5] The

---

[1] b. B.M. 74b.
[2] b. B.Q. 113b.
[3] b. B.M. 103b.
[4] Tos. B.M. 9:19.
[5] b. B.M. 105a. Since the sharecropper-*'aris*, as was noted above, had to give the landowner not less than two-thirds to three-quarters, the given formula has to do with the sharecropper-*qabellan*.

sharecropper sometimes even had to take the responsibility to realize the worth of the part of the harvest which belonged to the landowner, and moreover he was obliged to sell the crop in the most profitable manner for the landowner, for example, to sell vegetables not on the vegetable garden itself, but at the market where the price was much higher.[1] The sharecropper also fulfilled various duties which had no relation at all to the working of the lands which he sharecropped. So for example, it is said that the sharecropper is obliged to provide for feeding the domestic animals of the landholder and finding pasturage for them: "Usually the sharecropper submits himself to the landowner and brings him fodder."[2] Rava's sharecropper brought game to his table every day.[3]

In trying to increase their income by heavy exploitation of the sharecroppers, the landowners carefully watched so that the sharecroppers did not take anything beyond the part of the harvest set aside for them. If the sharecropper took even the most minimal amount of the fruit of the field and the orchard before the division of the harvest without the knowledge of the landowner, this was considered as simple thievery. Thus the sources say: "The sharecropper of R. Zevid stole a *qab* of barley. He pronounced him a good-for-nothing,"[4] unworthy of trust, unable to bear legal witness; in other words Zevid deprived him of his legal rights. Such cruel punishment also was meted out to another sharecropper by R. Zevid: "He stole a branch of unripe dates—[R. Zevid] pronounced him a good-for-nothing."[5] Only during the harvest or the gathering of the fruits did the sharecropper have the right to take a little bit of the harvest being gathered by him. Thus R. Naḥman (d. 320) declared that "a thief during Nisan [during the harvest in April] and a thief in Tishré [during the gathering of the fruit in October] is not called a thief; but only if the bit taken by him from the harvest is insignificant, and only if the processing of the grain and the fruits has already been completed."[6] When the harvest was already completed and processed and gathered together in one place, the landowner could more easily see that the sharecropper did not take anything without his knowledge. Landowners would accuse their sharecroppers of stealing for some

---

[1] Tos.
[2] b. B.M. 69a.
[3] b. Yoma 75b.
[4] b. Sanh. 26b.
[5] *Ibid.*
[6] b. Sanh. 26b.

reason or other. The following stories make this clear. The students of R. Huna (216-297) once expressed to him their surprise that he did not give his sharecropper the corresponding part of the dried-up branches of the grape vines. In justification of his deed R. Huna said that the sharecropper supposedly stole the dried branches from him: "Do you expect him [the sharecropper] to leave me some of them? He will steal all of them from me." The students of R. Huna were not satisfied with this answer from their teacher and reminded him of the folk-saying: "Steal from a thief and you will known its taste [that is, of the thing stolen]."[1] That is, a man who steals from a thief is also a thief. Abaye (280-338) once met his sharecropper, who was carrying a bundle of firewood. Abaye asked him, "Where are you carrying that?" The sharecropper answered him, "To my lord."[2] Abaye suspected he was intending to carry this bundle of firewood to his own home, so he said to him: "The teachers [= Samuel's Father] have already foreseen this [foreseen the possibility of such instances] when they said: 'Who looks after his properties daily will find an *istira*'." That is, he will preserve his worldly goods from theft by his sharecropper and increase in this way his income by many gold coins.

The statement "who looks over his land daily will find an *istira*" belongs to Mar Samuel (d. 254), who had on his land many sharecroppers. He did indeed oversee his fields daily.[3] Moreover he was much upset that he was not able to follow the example of his father, Abba bar Abba (second to third centuries) who lookedover his lands twice a day: "In relation to this, [Samuel said] I am, in comparison with my father, beer which has come from wine: my father looked over his lands twice a day, while I look over mine only once."[4] The landowners constantly watched after the work of their renters, systematically controlling it. For example, the landowner R. Ḥisda (217-309) once saw in the orchard which he had rented out palm trees among the grape-vines. He said to his sharecropper, "Pull out the palm trees, the grape-vines will acquire palm trees, but palm trees will not acquire grape-vines."[5] It was not possible to get grape-vines with the income from palm trees. Mar Samuel's sharecropper brought him dates, and when he ate them, he noticed in them the taste of wine.

---

[1] b. Ber. 5a.
[2] b. Hul. 105a.
[3] b. Hul. 105a.
[4] b. Hul. 105a.
[5] b. B.Q. 92a.

Samuel asked him, "What is this?" He answered him, "They stand among the grape vines." The date palms grow among the grape-vines, and for that reason the dates have the taste of wine. Samuel said to the sharecropper, "The date palms exhaust the wine [that is, the grape-vine] too much; pull out the date palm and, as proof, tomorrow bring me their roots."[1] The landowner showed understandably an especially great interest in the work of the sharecropper, since on the degree of its intensiveness depended the abundance of the harvest of the land-plot rented to him. Consequently the size of the portion of the harvest which the landowner would gain likewise depended on the land's fertility.

The size of the part of the harvest destined for the landowner, despite agreement at the time of the contract, called forth frequent disputes between the landowner and the sharecropper. Disputes arose in the cases of oral agreements or the loss of the written agreement. The sharecropper claims, "I was to get half." The owner says, "I allowed him one-third." Who should be believed? Rav Judah (218-298) says, "One trusts the owner." R. Naḥman says, "It is all according to the custom of the country."[2] The sharecropper should receive as much as it is the practice to give in any given place. In support of his opinion that it is always necessary to believe the landowner, reference is made to Mari, the son of the daughter of Samuel, who had transmitted the following saying from Abaye: "Even in an area where the sharecropper usually takes a half ... one believes the landowner [if he affirms that he had agreed with the sharecropper about offering him one-third of the harvest], since if the landholder would want to, he could say, 'He is not a sharecropper on the given plot of land but a hired workman of mine; he is my day-laborer,'"[3] who in general is not expected to receive anything from the harvest of a given land plot.

As noted, renters did not have the right to sow the lands rented by them according to their own judgment, but had, in choosing what grains to plant, to accommodate themselves to the local customs or to a condition earlier entered in the contract by the landholder. The breaking by the sharecropper of such a condition or of the local custom inevitably brought on disputes between landholders and share-croppers during the division of the harvest. One man, it is said, received land for sowing sesame, and sowed it with wheat [which

---
[1] Ibid.
[2] b. B.M. 110a.
[3] b. B.M. 110a.

usually brought less income than sesame]; but the wheat gave more [income] than sesame. Rabina said, "Let the landowner give the sharecropper the difference in the improvements,"[1] that is, the difference between the higher income received from sowing wheat, and the proposed income from sowing of sesame seed. R. Aḥa of Difti (fifth century) did not agree with Rabina. R. Aḥa explained, "Can it be that only the sharecropper has improved, but the land has not improved?"[2] Similarly, "A certain man received land for sesame seed; and he sowed it with wheat [which usually brings less profit, but exhausts the soil less]. The wheat yielded like sesame seed."[3] The sowing of wheat gave the same income as the sesame seed which was supposed to have been planted. R. Kahana (fourth to the fifth centuries) said, "The sharecropper deducts from him [the landholder] the exhausting of the soil."[4] The part of the harvest belonging to the landholder must be lessened in a sum corresponding to the difference between the exhausting of the soil from the sowing of sesame seed and its exhaustion from the sowing of the wheat. But R. Ashi objected to the decision of R. Kahana, referring to the proverb, "Let the land be exhausted, but let not its owner be exhausted."[5] The income of the landowner should not be in any measure lessened because of preserving the land from being exhausted. The proverb reflecting the views of the exploiters, and the decision of R. Ashi both point to the rapacious use of their landholdings by the landowners. They preserved their land from being exhausted only when it was possible to do this entirely at the expense of their renters, but never at the expense of their own income. For the sake of increasing income the landowners did not hesitate to exhaust the soil of their landholdings.

The renter had the right to use rented land not for the course of a whole year, but for only the extent of time necessary for producing one harvest. The time during which the renter could use the land plot rented by him depended on the character of the field rented. A renter could use an artificially watered field the whole year round, a naturally watered field only for the time necessary for going through the whole cycle of agricultural work necessary to produce one harvest: "If anyone rented a field *'bet hashlakhin'* [artificially watered] no less than

---

[1] b. B.M. 104b.
[2] *Ibid.*
[3] *Ibid.*
[4] b. B.M. 104b.
[5] *Ibid.*

twelve months the renter can use the rented plot; but if he rented a *bet haba'al* [a naturally watered field], he gathers his part of the theshing and goes away"[1] from the rented field. Distinguishing between the artificially-watered field and the naturally-watered one is because the latter usually gave only one harvest a year. The person who had rented such a field counted on only one harvest in a course of a year. During the time remaining after the harvest, the landowner had the right to use the field as pasturage for domestic animals or for other purposes. The artificially-watered field gave two or three harvests a year, and the person who rented such a field could use it the whole year round for sequential sowing; the right of the renter to use such a field the whole year round did not require any special agreements in the rent contract. In order to lengthen the period during which they themselves could make use of the field, the landowners often forced the renters of the naturally-watered field to harvest before the grain had had time enough to ripen completely. For permission to use the field up until the full ripening of the harvest, the landowners would require a special, additional payment. Thus, Rava (d. 352) received from his renters a payment one and one-half times greater than that agreed upon, because he gave the land for their use for a period of one month longer than that which was customary.[2] Students of Rava reproached him once because of this and accused him of an illegal action: "The students said to Rava '... everyone takes as rent payment for a land plot of a certain size four *kors* of grain and gets rid of his renters from the rented field in Nisan [April]; but Mar [the teacher] waits for them [allows them to use the field] up to Iyyar [the month following Nisan] and takes as rent six *kors* of grain.' Rava said to them, 'You [that is, those who take four *kors*] are acting illegally ... you chase the renters away in Nisan, and you cause them a great loss [since you force them to gather the harvest which has not yet had time to ripen]. I on the other hand wait for them until Iyyar, and I bring to them by this means a large profit.'"[3]

Rent contract was concluded usually in written form.[4] Besides the exact fulfillment of the conditions of the contract, the renter had to observe the existing "local customs" with regard to working the land: the character and time of fertilizing, plowing, sowing, the forms of

---

[1] Tos. B.M. 9:2.
[2] b. B.M. 73a.
[3] *Ibid.*
[4] *Shetar khakirut* is a rent contract, and *shetar 'arisut* is a sharecropping agreement.

reaping, the gathering of the harvest and so on. In the case of breaking any conditions of the contract or not observing the "local customs," the landholder could cancel the contract and take the land away from the renters. Using this excuse, the landowner often chased the renters off the fields even in the middle of the year, thus depriving them of the fruits of their long and heavy labor and subjecting their families to starvation. Just such a fate befell the renters if it seemed for some reason to the landowner that they did not show sufficient responsibility for the lands rented by them, worked them insufficiently, or carelessly treated the responsibilities they had taken on themselves. Such accusations were made when, thanks to the measures undertaken to improve the lands by the renters, the abundance of the harvest was increased, and the landowner had for that reason the possibility of renting the land to a new renter on conditions more profitable for himself.[1] The following story is characteristic: "R. Ḥisda (217-309) had a share-cropper who divided up the harvest accurately and exactly, was careful to watch that the landholder did not give him a false weight, and did not diminish the part of the harvest which belonged to him. This was not to the taste of the landholder, who wanted to dispose of the harvest personally, and the sharecropper was punished by depriving him of his sharecropper's share. R. Ḥisda chased him from the land and said, 'And preserve for the righteous man the riches of the sinner.'"[2] To force renters and sharecroppers to work harder, landholders promised to reduce the land rent so as to increase the share of the harvest if the sharecroppers would work more carefully and water their fields more frequently. Thus we have a story of one landholder who said to his sharecropper at the time of concluding the contract, "All the sharecroppers draw water for watering thrice [water the fields worked by them three times] and eat [receive for their use] a quarter [one-quarter part of the harvest], but you draw four times [water the fields four times] and eat [receive for your use] a third."[3] But the landowners would renege on their promises to raise the amount of the part of the harvest for the sharecroppers.

The landowners broke up land into small plots in order to rent them to the largest number of renters. The latter therefore had at their disposal land-plots so limited in size that working them gave even in the best cases the possibility of a poor existence. The renters were

---

[1] ŠBḤ is, in Aramaic, ŠBTʾ.
[2] *Ibid.* The words spoken by R. Ḥisda are Proverbs 19:32.
[3] b. Giṭ. 74b.

in an especially difficult position in years of poor harvest. The renters had to pay the rent in full if the poor harvest touched only the plots rented by them or the region immediately adjacent. Only in the case of a generally poor harvest, "when most of the fields of the region were burned up"[1] or "when the fields on each of the four sides of the rented field were burned up"[2] did the landholder have to lower the land rent agreed upon by the contract. But he did not have entirely to reduce it. The agreed-upon amount of the rent was not lowered when the adjacent river or canal flowing by the field would dry up. In such instances the landowner would say to the renter: "You should bring water in a pail."[3] That is, if the natural sources dried up, the renter was obliged to take care of watering. The sharecropper had to complete his work on the land to harvest the field, no matter what the quality of the harvest. Further, if the sowing did not produce sufficient results, or if for any reason the plants perished, the sharecropper was obliged in such instances to sow a second time during that same year: "The sharecropper sows once and sows again."[4] Certain law makers considered that the sharecropper was obliged in such instances to sow even for a third time.[5] Moreover the question of how many times the sharecropper is obliged to repeat his sowing concerns only those instances when "they sowed and it grew, but the locusts ate it up."[6] If they sowed and nothing grew, the landowner had the right to say to the sharecropper, "Sow and keep sowing,"[7] until the sowing does produce results. If the field was rented for a period of several years, then the landowner could force the renter to sow also during the second year, despite the fact that in the first year nothing grew.

The renters also were in a difficult position when, because of the lack of resources to buy seed or acquire the necessary instruments of production, they were not able to work the rented land and had to leave it to lie fallow. Contracts concerning rent took account of such instances: "If I leave my land to lie fallow and do not work it, I will pay the best price."[8] The renter was obliged to buy corresponding grain of the best quality and to pay the land-rent with it to the land-

---

[1] b. B.M. 105b.
[2] *Ibid.*
[3] b. B.M. 103b, 104a.
[4] b. B.M. 106b.
[5] *Ibid.*
[6] *Ibid.*
[7] *Ibid.*
[8] M. B.M. 9:3.

holder at the price agreed upon in the contract. If the land is unworked, "the field is appraised as to how much it will make [if it is worked], and the sharecropper gives correspondingly"[1] the agreed-upon part of the harvest to the landholder. Some landholders forced the renters to accept in the contract even more difficult conditions. In case the lands remained unworked, a significant sum in the form of a fine, over and above the land rent required, had to be paid, as in the following instance: "One man rented land as a sharecropper from his neighbor and (on concluding the agreement) said to the landholder: 'If I leave it to lie fallow, I will give you [as a fine] a thousand *zuz*.' He left one-third of the land to lie fallow. The judges of the city of Nehardea said, 'It is expected that he [the sharecropper] would give him [the landowner] three hundred thirty-three and one-third *zuz*,'[2] and they sentenced the sharecropper to pay the landowner one-third of the agreed upon sum of the fine, corresponding to that part of the field which he left unworked."

The renters could acquire grain and pay the other necessary agricultural expenses and rent when there was no real harvest at all only by seeking loans, most often from the landowner himself. The latter would deduct everything that he had given in loan to the renter either in money or grain at usurious interest, thus increasing the debt. An exception to the general depositions effective in Talmudic law concerning giving loans at interest was made for renters: "If anyone should rent a field from his neighbor for ten *kors* of wheat a year and says to the landowner, 'Give me [in loan] two hundred *zuz*, and I will improve [the field] and pay you twelve *kors* of wheat a year'—this is permitted."[3] It is not considered usury. The exception to the general law forbidding giving grain on loan[4] is made in connection with the renters only when they take grain on credit for sowing and not for food. The renters thus fell into a slave-like dependence, taking grain for sowing and also for their own food. These debts were collected by the landholder after the harvest from the part destined for the renters. As a result the renters had only an insignificant portion of the harvest; they were forced, immediately after finishing the reaping and gathering of the harvest, once again to seek loans from the landowner in order to feed themselves and to meet the expenses of working the lands.

---

[1] b. B.M. 104b.
[2] *Ibid.*
[3] b. B.M. 69b.
[4] M. B.M. 5:8-9, b. B.M. 74b.

The renters did not have any possibility of refusing the land plots no matter how heavy and enslaving the conditions of the rent might be. Tied to the landowners by numerous and constantly growing debts, the renters turned out to be tied to the land rented by them. They were in fact deprived of the possibility of leaving this land and seeking to work the land of other landholders. They were in full serfdom.

The variety in rent was made up by renting tilled or completely unworked plots of land to a planter (ŠTL') for raising a fruit orchard. Such a sharecropper received one-half of the harvest of fruit grown by him in the orchard, in the manner of the sharecropper-*qabbelan* and not one-third or one-fourth, like the sharecropper-'*aris*. Similarly, the renter-fruit grower had to give to the landowner as land-rent a lesser quantity of fruit and a lesser sum of money in comparison with that which the ordinary renter would give.[1] Despite this the position of such a renter was more difficult than that of the ordinary sharecropper. All expenses necessary for cultivating the orchard, sometimes quite significant ones, were borne by the fruit grower. He had for several years to do all work connected with the raising of fruit trees, watering them and digging, without receiving reward for his labor for all this time. Not having any resources of his own, the fruit grower was forced to take loans, most often from the owner of the land under cultivation. As a result, from the very beginning he fell into complete dependence on the landowner. But the position of the fruit grower was not much better even after the orchard had begun to bear fruit. The fruit growers had at their disposal extremely small land plots. The fruit garden, even after the trees began to bear fruit, required systematic investment and constant hard work on the part of the fruit grower. As time passed the dependence of the fruit grower on the landowner kept increasing. No matter how burdensome the conditions of the rent, he was deprived of every possibility of refusing further work on the land he had planted. To be sure, if the renter-fruit grower left the orchard, the landowner had to pay him one-half "of the improvement." That is, half of that sum by which the value of the given land plot was increased as a result of its having been planted and turned into an orchard. But this half "of the improvement" went to the fruit grower only when he left the land plot with the *agreement* of the landowners! Only when the departure of the fruit grower was profitable to the land-

---

[1] b. B.M. 109b.

holder was the renter compensated. If the fruit grower left the land contrary to the wish of the landholder, he would receive only one-sixth "of the improvement".[1]

But the fruit grower who left his garden rarely succeeded in receiving even his sixth part "of the improvement." If the landholder said that the sharecropper carelessly went about his duties, looked after the land badly, or watered it insufficiently, or caused damage to the orchard, the fruit grower was deprived of the right to receive his part "of the improvement." He left the land without any compensation at all. The landowner could always make such an accusation against the fruit grower when it appeared to him profitable to cancel the contract and get rid of the fruit grower. He could always find a basis for not paying compensation to the fruit grower. The landowner could take as his own, at no cost, the results of the labor of many years on the part of the fruit grower and all of the investment which the fruit grower had put into the land. Thus: "Ronia, the fruit grower of Rabina, did harm [to an orchard.] Rabina got rid of him. Ronia came to Rava and said to him, 'Look, teacher, at what Rabina has done with me.' Rava said to him, 'He has done well.' Ronia said to him, 'He warned me [that in case of causing harm he would get rid of me].' Rava said to him, 'It is not necessary to warn ... it is considered that the fruit grower is already as though forewarned.'"

Some landowners tried in advance to assure themselves of the possibility of cancelling the contract and getting rid of the fruit grower when he should be no longer needed. For this purpose they forced their fruit growers to enter into the contract that if they caused harm to the orchard they would "get rid of themselves." They would have to leave the orchard, and by this it was understood that the fruit grower would leave the garden without payment to him of any compensation. "A certain fruit grower said to the landowner [while concluding the contract], 'If I cause harm, I will leave.' He afterwards caused harm. Rav Judah said, 'He leaves without receiving his improvements.'"[2] The fruit grower himself who, in the case of cancelling the contract, received nothing in repayment for his labor and investment in growing the orchard, could never decide to leave the orchard.

Furthermore the orchard grown by the renter did not necessarily go after the death of the fruit grower to his heirs. R. Joseph had a fruit grower. The fruit grower died and left five sons-in-law. R.

---
[1] b. B.M. 109a.
[2] *Ibid.*

Joseph thought, "Up to this time there was one sharecropper, now five ... will rely on each other and will cause me harm." R. Joseph said to the heirs of the fruit grower, "If you take [your improvements] and go—good, and if not I will get rid of you without (paying) the improvements."[1] According to the opinion of Rav Judah (218-298), "If the fruit grower should die, the heirs leave without improvements."[2]

VI. Workmen and Agricultural Day Workers

Not all of the small landowners deprived of their land were successful in remaining on their former plots as renters or to rent the land of other owners. Many of them were forced to find other sources of food for themselves. A part of them tried to find additional work outside their craft, or in small trade or as hired hands. The rest became workmen and agricultural day workers. Many of the small landholders and renters who continued to carry on their own farm work also entered the ranks of agricultural day workers, for their farms were so modest that they could not feed their own families. The hired hands were of various types: day workers, seasonal workers, permanent ones, and "entrepreneurs," who agreed for a certain sum to fulfill some agricultural function, for example, to plow a certain land plot, to sow it, to reap, and to take the harvest to the threshing floor, to thresh the grain from a certain land plot, to winnow, and so on.

The permanent day laborer, who worked for one and the same landowner a rather lengthy period of time and who lived permanently in his house was called a *sakhir*,[3] hired hand, or a *laqit*,[4] gatherer. The *sakhir* was hired for a fixed time—for a year, or two, or three—and had some sort of personal property of his own; he possibly also owned his tools of trade. The *laqit* lived at the house of the landowner as a permanent day worker, and had no personal property of his own. Even his clothes were received from the landholder.[5] The name *laqit* shows that this category of hired laborers was recruited from the poorest stratum of the population. The day laborer did not have any means at all and in order to feed himself was forced to gather the

---

[1] b. B.M. 109a.
[2] *Ibid.*
[3] From the verb SKR—"to hire."
[4] b. Eruv. 64a, b. Shevuot 46b, b. B.M. 110b (from the verb LQT—"gather," "gather up.")
[5] b. Ket. 54a.

gleanings left after the harvest *(leqeṭ)*. But even the day laborers *(sakhir)* were taken from entirely landless, former small landholders, renters who had lost their own property and all hope of restoring it. Both the *laqiṭ* and the *sakhir*, because of their material condition, had no possibility of leaving their landholding employers. They were enslaved.

Temporary hired laborers, *poʻalin*,[1] were hired daily, or for a week or a month. Many were hired not for a fixed time, but for a fixed payment to do some agricultural work, for example to plow and sow a certain plot of land and so on. Such hired workers, indicated by the term *qabbelan* (entrepreneur), received for the most part not payment in money but a fixed portion of the harvest reaped by them or the grain threshed by them. Temporary agricultural workers were hired primarily for various irrigation jobs,[2] drawing water, watering fields,[3] to plow,[4] to weed,[5] to reap,[6] to gather fruit,[7] to protect the fields and streams,[8] and so on. Guards for the protection of the fields and the streams were hired often by all the landowners of a certain community.[9] The temporary hired worker frequently found himself out of work, especially after the completion of the season. The expression *poʻel baṭel*,[10] unemployed worker, occurs frequently. In expectation of demand for their labor, the unemployed crowded into special "markets" set aside for them in each city. Here the landowners would come early in the morning to hire the workers they needed: "Go, look, how many unemployed there are at the market."[11] Hired workers had to move from place to place. The sources speak about such workers "who just came," for instance in connection with discussion about the time of the beginning and end of the working day: "Let us see what is the custom ... and let us see, where they came from?"[12] The working day had to be regulated by the local customs of the city or of the

---

[1] "Poʻel" (worker) from the verb "paʻal" (to work, make); occurs mostly in plural "poʻalim."
[2] b. B.M. 76a.
[3] *Ibid.* 77a.
[4] *Ibid.* 76a.
[5] *Ibid.* 89b.
[6] y. B.M. 6:1, Tos. Peʾah 3:1.
[7] b. B.M. 89b.
[8] b. B.M. 73a, 93a.
[9] *Ibid.*
[10] b. B.M. 76b, 77a.
[11] b. Ber. 17b.
[12] b. B.M. 83a.

region in which the employer lived or from which the given hired workman came. In the given instance it is a question of "a new city," where firmly established local customs did not exist, the hired workers were *naquté* (NQT'Y) who came from various localities.[1] Payment for the work, especially of hired laborers, was subject to significant variations, dropping by one-quarter or more of the usual payment.[2] Hired workers were poverty stricken and had no money to live on. They therefore were permitted to use social aid and any alms set aside for the poor.

In certain localities landowners supervised the daily food so the workers would not waste time on eating.[3] They were present while hired hands were fed; they sometimes ate together with them. Their presence would speed up the eating. The food was quite poor, bread with a porridge made of grain husks.[4] But the cost of this poor food often covered in full the daily pay of the hired workers.[5] Those hired workers from among the small landowners *(baʿalé batim)* usually required much higher pay than other hired workmen. When a landowner ordered someone to go and hire workers for him at a payment of three *denars* a day, his factor hired workers for four *denars* a day.[6] Some suggested that such disputes be resolved on the basis of local custom: "Let them look (they said) at how the workers of a given locality are hired." Others objected that it will not always be possible to decide the question on the basis of local customs alone: "There are workmen who are hired for four (*denars* a day) and others for three. Therefore the workmen can say to the landowner, 'If he had not said to us during the hiring 'for four,' we would have tried to be hired by somebody else for four,'" If the workers owned property, they could say to the hirer, "If you do not say to us that we will be hired for four, we should be ashamed to hire ourselves out."[7]

Small landowners, having their own property, however modest and insufficient for feeding the family, nevertheless had a greater leeway. They were hired when the demand for labor was increased. The workers deprived of their own property had to agree to any conditions of payment for their labor.

---

[1] b. B.M. 86b.
[2] b. B M. 76a, 77a.
[3] b. B.M. 91b.
[4] b. Ber. 16a, 46a.
[5] b. Ber. 16a.
[6] b. B.M. 76a.
[7] b. B.M. 76a.

The employers could at any time reject hired workers. When the rejection of the hired worker occurred before the worker had begun his work, the hirer was not bound to pay him in return for any time lost by him.[1] For the day worker, however, the loss of work entailed the loss of an entire working day; having missed the established time for hiring day workers, he no longer could find other work. But even if the refusal to hire occurred after the hired workman had begun to work, the hirer still was bound to pay in compensation only a certain part of the agreed upon sum, "as for doing nothing."[2] Even such partial compensation to workers let go was not paid, since the pretext for the rejection was some earlier circumstance unforeseen by the hirer. For example Rava said, "If someone should hire workmen for digging a canal or a ditch for irrigation, and suddenly it began to rain and the canal filled with water, then if the workmen had looked over the land the night before, the loss is the workmen's."[3] If the workers had acquainted themselves earlier with the place where they were to work, the hirer was not bound to pay them compensation for lost time, since they themselves should have been able to foresee the possibility of what happened. Rava further said, "If someone should hire the laborers for drawing water for the watering of the fields and it should rain, the loss is the workers'."[4] "If someone should hire workers for the drawing of water, and the water in the rivers stopped during the day, and if it usually does not happen that the water stops in the river, the loss is the workers'. If the water stops, then, if they are inhabitants of the locality, the loss is the workers'. If they are not inhabitants of the locality, the loss is the landowners'."[5] The employer could refer to "unforeseen circumstances" and did not have to pay to hire workmen. The employer thus could get rid of his hired workmen without payment of compensation whenever he changed his mind on the proposed work, or, because of falling prices for field hands, could find other workers for less money.

Formally the hired workmen were able to change their minds about working.[6] Bourgeois researchers[7] have tried to prove that hired work-

---

[1] b. B.M. 76b.
[2] b. B.M. 76b.
[3] b. B.M. 76b.
[4] b. B.M. 77a.
[5] *Ibid.*
[6] b. B.Q. 116b, b. B.M. 10a, 15a.
[7] See, for example, Farbstein. *Das Recht der unfreien und freien Arbeiter nach judischtalmudischem Recht.* (Frankfurt a. M., 1896) pp. 56, 57.

ers had the same rights as the employers and could refuse to work. But the hired laborer did not have any possibility of making use of this "right." Nor could he break his agreement with his employer. It was difficult to find work, and having found work, the laborer hardly would refuse it and lose a working day. The worker bore full responsibility for the loss caused to the employer because of the interruption of the work. Abba Arika, to whom is ascribed the law that "the laborer can refuse to work even during the day,"[1] required the worker to see to the end of the work begun by him and to hire at this own expense workers to bring it to conclusion at any price.[2]

Bearers and teamsters of trade goods were responsible for the condition of the goods they transported. Ḥiyya b. Joseph ruled the carriers responsible for the condition and preservation of wine vessels transported by them. He defined when and under what conditions the bearers are responsible for breaking wine vessels and were obliged to compensate the owner for losses.[3] Two carriers broke a wine vessel while transporting the wine vessels belonging to Raba bar bar Ḥana. Raba bar bar Ḥana took away the carriers' clothing. The latter came to Rava to complain and said to him: "We are poor, we have worked the whole day, we are hungry and we have nothing." Rava ordered Raba bar bar Ḥana to return the clothing to the carriers and to pay them for their labor. Raba asked, "Is this the law?" Rava answered that according to law it is true that it is not required, but that sometimes one must act "above the law."[4]

VII. NEW FORMS OF EXPLOITATION OF THE LABOR OF SLAVES AND THEIR GRADUAL BINDING TO THE LAND

Large estates of the landholding gentry were worked by slaves. Attesting to this is the story about the sale of "Daskarta"[5] estates together with the slaves who worked them.[6] When something is found by a buyer in grain bought directly from the landowner, then the thing must be returned. In discussion of this law, the question is raised, "Can it be that the owner [of the field] himself threshed the

---

[1] b. B.Q. 116b, b. B.M. 76b.
[2] b. B.M. 76b.
[3] b. B.M. 83a.
[4] b. B.M. 83a.
[5] Daskarta is the Persian word meaning "city," "settlement," "village," "a castle surrounded by services."
[6] b. Git. 40a.

grain?"¹ The seller of grain was in most cases a large and affluent landholder. R. Naḥman affirms that the landholder in fact did not personally thresh the grain, "but threshed the grain with the hands of his male and female slaves" but "their hands are the same as the hands of the landlord himself."² The discussion of the seizure of others' lands begins with these words: "If he will take his own slaves, and go into the field of his neighbor and say: 'It is mine ....'"³ Thus for the practical ownership of lands, slaves are necessary. Rava said, "By these three actions landowners lose their lands: Whoever grants freedom to his slaves ..."⁴ Freeing slaves brings on the ruin of the owner because there is no one to work his land. The appearance of a great demand for agricultural products for the internal market and for export and the beginning of the development of new productive forces made the labor of the slaves in its old form unprofitable. This hastened the disintegration of the slave-owing system, necessitating a change in the means of production. Slave labor is characterized as inefficient. Slaves are lazy, and not very productive. "Ten measures of sleep came down onto the earth—nine (measures) the slaves took and all the rest (took) one."⁵ R. Naḥman said, "A slave is not worth the bread for his belly."⁶

Marx wrote, "The development of trade and of trade capital everywhere develops production in the direction of commercial value, increases its size, gives it more variety, lends it a cosmopolitan character, and develops money into universal currency. Therefore trade everywhere influences in a more or less distintegrating fashion those organizations of production which it overtakes and which in all of its various forms are directed in the main toward the production of consumer goods. But how far that disintegration of the old means of production advances depends first of all on its stability and its internal structure."⁷

The disintegration of the slave-owning system in Iraq began as early as the first century A.D. The development of trade, especially after the middle of the second century, contributed to the process of disintegration of the slave-owning means of production. This process,

---

[1] b. B.M. 27a.
[2] *Ibid.*
[3] b. B.Q. 112b.
[4] b. Git. 38b.
[5] b. Qid. 49b.
[6] b. B.Q. 97a, b. B.M. 64b.
[7] K. Marx, *Das Kapital*, Vol. I. K. Marx & F. Engels, *Works* Vol. XIX, part 1, p.359.

common for Iraq as a whole, found its expression in Talmudic literature. One of the evidences of the disintegration of the slave-owning means of production was the tendency to free slaves, to turn them into "free" workers, the exploitation of whom would be more efficient. Certain strata of landowners opposed this development by forbidding the mass emancipation of slaves. Mar Samuel said, "Anyone who frees his slaves breaks God's commandment."[1] These landholders, many of whom were slave-owners, feared that widespread emancipation of slaves would destroy the slave-owning economy. But all the attempts to forbid the emancipation of slaves came to nothing. This is attested by the fact that in the third and fourth centuries were many localities completely settled by freed slaves. Rava, in the struggle against mixing free men with former slaves, stated in the city of Maḥoza, where he was head of the Talmudical school, "The Belites, Denites, Telaites, and Melaites, and Ṣegaites [inhabitants of the settlements Bela, Dena, Tela, Mela, and Ṣega] are all worthless."[2] They are all former slaves, and free men should not fraternize with them. These are all former slaves or their heirs; otherwise there would be no necessity for warning free men about the true character of the population of the given localities. They are "worthless," "come from slaves," or are "descendents of *netinim*." Real slaves are called such. Thus Rav Judah spoke in Pumbedita, "Ada and Jonathan are slaves, Judah bar Papa is a bastard, but Batti bar Ṭuvyah, because of his tribe, has not taken out his manumission paper."[3] Therefore he must be considered a slave now and henceforth, until he protects himself with the corresponding document.

Such a radical measure as full emancipation could be undertaken only by part of the slave owners. Most tried to preserve the old slave-owning system by exploiting the labor of slaves through new methods, corresponding to the new economic conditions. Slave owners settled slaves on land plots divided up to be worked individually. Moreover, originally the slave owners gave slaves produce for a certain amount of time.[4] Such provisions are called PRS or PRNSH.[5] Usually the term

---

[1] b. Ber. 47b, Git. 38b.
[2] b. Qid 70b.
[3] *Ibid.*
[4] The time period usually depended on the extent to which the slave owner was satisfied with the work of the slave. The sources say, by the way, that it is much more profitable to the slave when his master gives him his due over a longer time, since the "millstones grind (it gets lost during threshing) from the *kor* (large grain measure) the same as from a *qab* (a small measure); dough eats it up (it gets lost during baking the bread) from a *kor* as well as a *qab*." (b. Ta'anit 19b)
[5] b. Ber. 34, b. Eruv. 72b, 73a, b. Ta'anit 25b, b. B.B. 25a.

peras is translated by the word *gift*.¹ "When a slave serves his master as he should, he requires his *peras* from him."² "The slave requires his *peras* only close to the time established for giving out the *peras*."³ "When a slave takes his *peras* from his master, turns around and bows down, that is a sign of his gratitude." "Like a slave who begs his lord for his *peras*." The lord said to his overseer, "Give to him, that I should not hear his voice,"⁴ or he would say, "Wait in giving him his *peras* until the slave is wearied, and only then give to him."⁵ If *peras* meant gift, the slave would not dare to ask for it with such insistence, much less require it.

Peras means provisions given to the slave after a fixed period of time. This is indicated by the following excerpt, in which the words *peras* and *parnas* means "provisions" or "food stuffs." "When a slave serves his master in full measure, he (the slave) requires his *peras* from him." Said R. Joshua, "(Only) from the time that the slave serves his master in full measure and the master is satisfied with him does the slave have the right to require *parnas* from the master."⁶ We see thus that the term *peras* and *parnas* mean "provisions" or "food stuffs." So too: a man had "five wives, who received *peras* from their husband, and five slaves, who received *peras* from their master."⁷ In context *peras* can be understood *only* as provisions given out for a fixed period of time. Even those who translate *peras* as *remuneration, payment*,⁸ have not understood the social meaning of the term under discussion. They therefore have misunderstood precisely what kind of remuneration the slave receives.

The provisions received by the slave were also a reward for working on the plot of land set aside for him by the landowner. The slave may ask for it since it was his single source of existence.⁹ However, the system of payment for slave labor by giving a certain quantity of

---

¹ See, for example, J. Levy, *Wörterbuch über die Talmudim und Midraschim* IV, 124.
² y. Taʿanit 1:1.
³ *Ibid.*
⁴ b. B.B. 25a.
⁵ b. Taʿanit 25b.
⁶ y. Taʿanit 1:1.
⁷ b. Eruv. 73a.
⁸ K. Marti, G. Beer, *Abot, Die Mishna herausgegeben von G. Beer.* (Giessen, 1927).
⁹ The attempt to derive the work "peras" from the Greek Φόρος has been unsuccessful; in our understanding, "peras" is derived from the Hebrew verb "paras," "to break off," and its original meaning was "a broken off piece," " a part of the portion." The origin of the term can be explained by the fact that in the beginning, such a slave was given his due in the form of baked bread.

produce, independent of the results of his labor and outside of any connection with his productivity, did not involve the slave in the productiveness of his labor. Therefore, instead of giving fixed provisions, the slave-owners began to offer part of the harvest from the plot worked by him. The slave had to work harder and more carefully, and to improve the quality of his work. If the share of the harvest was insufficient for the slave's livelihood, the slave owner was not obliged to feed him.[1] "The slave who is not worth the bread for his belly—why is he needed by his master and mistress?"[2] A further inducement for the slave was that some sort of "extras" might remain, to accrue to his means for improving the land and also raise his personal material condition.

A further step in binding the slaves to the land was to offer the slave the right to use the harvest of the land worked by him in its entirety. The slave-owner would receive rent. But at the same time that he worked on the plot for his personal use, the slave was obliged to work for a certain number of days on the fields of the slave owner. This is the sense of the phrase, "Work for me, and I shall not feed you."[3] That is, working for the slave owner during the course of a certain time in the year, or a certain number of days per week or per month, the slave received nothing for all this work, and had to feed himself exclusively on the income from the plot reserved for his use by the slave owner.

It is well to consider in more detail the problem of "surpluses" (H'DPH) which the slave might have from the plot set aside for him, after he had satisfied all the requirements. The sources indicate that under all the various conditions of the slave "holding the land," the "surpluses" belonged to the slave owner. This seemed so self-evident that this puzzled question was asked: Why was it necessary

---

[1] b. Git. 12a.
[2] *Ibid.*
[3] Bourgeois historians, not knowing how to penetrate the essence of a given disposition, understood it in a literal sense. The slave owner sometimes forced his slave to work for his own keep, not giving him any kind of share, thus consigning him to starvation. In order to rehabilitate the slave-owners from the accusation of cruel treatment of the slaves, these historians, referring to the statements in the sources concerning slaves, maintain that the right of the slave owner to say "Work for me, but I will not feed you," was only theoretical in character, and that it was invoked in practice extremely rarely. As we have shown, this disposition had nothing to do with either cruelty or "humanity," but only reflected the new productive relationship between the slave owners and their slaves.

to have a special disposition on the fact that a surplus in a slave's income above his own portion belonged to the slave owner, when that is self-evident? The following answer was given to that question: One might think that if he [the lord] does not have [a surplus], he [the lord] should not take from him."[1] Sometimes it was even determined beforehand what the quality of the slave's food should be, and to what extent he has the right to enjoy the income from his work, and also that he keep as much surplus as possible, although it legally belonged to the slave owner.

However, the right of the slave owner to the surplus was only conditional, similar to the right of the slave owner to the *pekulii* of the slave, and meant only that in expending the surplus, the slave had, to a certain extent, to take into consideration the slave owner's interest. In actual fact, the "surplus" remained entirely in the hands of the slave as his *pekulii*. Nevertheless, the slave owner was extremely interested in having the slave keep as much surplus as possible, so that greater savings would pile up. These "surpluses," or savings, allowed the slave to improve his agriculture, acquire better means of production, fertilize the soil of his plot and so on. All these measures on the part of the slave raised the productivity of his land plot, which, in turn, automatically raised the returns of the slave owner from the slave's plot by raising the size of the part of the harvest belonging to him.

All the foregoing shows that in Iraq at the time under consideration, some quite new productive relations between masters and slaves were established, relations which recall the corvée and poll-tax of the feudal period.[2] On such bases, whether corvée or poll-tax, the landowners let the slaves work on the side. In connection with discussion of the

---

[1] b. Git. 12a.

[2] Fustel de Coulanges, investigating the character of "slave holding in Rome," comes to the following conclusions: "From the first centuries of the Empire, landowners had recourse to various methods of running their estates. One of these was to place slaves onto especially divided plots, as though they were tenant farmers. Sometimes they were slaves from the outside, and sometimes they came from the number of the landowner's own slaves. In the course of a long time, the most widespread method of exploiting the big estates in the Roman Empire was by working the land with all the slaves taken together *(familia rustica)*. But parallel to this method, another began to be established little by little, which appeared at first rather rarely, as an exception but which slowly began to spread, and finally predominated. This method was to place an individual slave on an especially portioned off plot and entrust him with working it, with a reservation of using the harvest subject to certain conditions."(*Rimskii Kolonat* [St. Petersburg, 1908] pp. 56, 59).

question of responsibility of the renter for care of domestic animals rented by him for his work is the disposition that if the owner of the domesticated animal hired himself out along with the animal, then the person hiring bore no responsibility. R. Ilish (fourth century) asked in such a case: "If someone says to his slave, 'Go and hire yourself out with my animal,' then what?"[1]—that is, is the hirer in this case responsible for the safety of the beast, as in the usual case of hiring the beast without its owner, or does the presence of the slave of the owner free him from responsibility? Rava answered: "It goes without saying that the hand of a slave is like the hand of his master,"[2] that is, in such a case, the hirer is freed from responsibility for the safety of the beast. The expression "Go and hire yourself out with my animal" shows that slave owners often let slaves go for work on the side, having supplied them with the tools of production, and obliging them to do so through the corvée and the poll-tax.

However, despite the process of distintegration of the slave-owning system of the period we can point also to times in which slavery fell into recidivism [Translator's Note: This means that there were relapses in the historical process of the disintegration of slavery. Despite gradual disintegration, at times there was an increase of slavery.] when the ruling class strove to acquire slaves, the number of whom was increased from the ranks of debtors without means, those who did not pay the poll-tax, or people "who conducted themselves in an unbecoming manner." Thus the landholders during the reign of Shapur II (309-379) made use of the Iranian state law, according to which a man who did not pay his poll-tax would be enslaved by the person who would pay the tax for him. Among the enslavers were many students of law. R. Papa (300-375) turned to Rava, the head of the school of Mahoza, with a complaint, "Look, master, [said R. Papa to Rava], those teachers of the law give people money for (paying off) the poll-tax and enslave them."[3] Rava answered him that they do so quite correctly, because of the teaching of R. Sheshet, "The tax rolls[4] of those obliged to pay the tax lie in the archives of the king, and the king has said, 'Whoever did not pay the poll-tax, let him be enslaved by the one who gives the poll-tax for him.'"[5] Members of the family

---

[1] b. B.M. 96a.
[2] *Ibid.*
[3] b. B.M. 73b.
[4] MWHRQ' is the Persian MHRH.
[5] *Ibid.*

of Papa bar Abba made extensive use of the practice of paying off the poll-tax for, then enslaving, people who had no means. R. Papa asked Rava whether a special document of manumission was needed for people enslaved in this way, should they be set free. Rava answered that in case of manumission a document of manumission is necessary for the enslaved non-payers of the poll-tax.[1] Consequently the enslaved non-payers of the tax were looked upon like real slaves, not as people who were temporarily working off the tax which had been paid for them.

Further, Jews in Bé Miksé borrowed money from gentiles. When the time for payment came, they had no money, so then the money-lenders "came and took them away" into slavery.[2] They turned to R. Huna to help buy them out of slavery. He refused, for this was not the first time they had fallen into slavery in such a way. The law forbids buying out of slavery any man who, after he has once before been bought out of slavery from a gentile, sells himself to the gentile for a second time.[3] This story shows that the enslavement of debtors without means was a frequent phenomenon. The inhabitants of whole settlements were enslaved for non-payment of debts.

It is not surprising therefore that "a man would be better off in case of extreme need to sell his own daughter, than to borrow money at interest. The daughter gradually lessens the sum necessary for buying her out of slavery. The debt on the other hand grows."[4] Slavery results from borrowing money at interest, and selling oneself into slavery is the inevitable consequence.[5] The money-lenders not only enslaved debtors without means, but also "caught" slaves, in general. Mishnaic law forbade buying out of slavery any man who enslaved himself to a gentile: "Whoever sells himself to a gentile is not ransomed, but his children and his wife are ransomed" (M. Git. 4:9). The Babylonian rabbis mitigated this law by saying it applied only to those who have already sold themselves "twice or thrice." Those who sold themselves for the first time must be ransomed. This resulted from the mass character of the enslavement of debtors without means.

Joseph, father of Rava, "caught the slaves of his debtors and forced

---

[1] b. Yev. 46a.
[2] b. Git. 46b.
[3] b. Git. 46b.
[4] b. Qid. 20a.
[5] *Ibid.*

them to work for him."[1] Rava asked his father, Joseph, on what basis he did so. Joseph referred first, to the statement of R. Naḥman, "The slave is not worth the bread for his belly."[2] Then he quoted Rabbah, "If anyone seizes the slave of his neighbor and forces him to work for him, then he is free of all need to compensate the owner of the slave, because it is desirable to the slave owner that the slave be forced to work, in order not to ruin himself."[3] That is, the slave would not become a lazy man. The son rejected this answer, pointing out to him that if it is possible "to seize" the slaves of other people, then it is not possible to do this in regard to one's own debtors: "This is like usury," which is forbidden by law.[4]

"They seized" not only the slaves of their own debtors and slaves in general, but also free persons of certain categories under the pretext that they were supposedly "useless," that they "conducted themselves unbecomingly." Seʿoram, brother of Rava, used to "grab useless people and harness them to his [Rava's] palanquin."[5] Rava fully approved of the act of his brother and said to him, "You do well, for thus did the lawgivers teach, 'If you notice that someone conducts himself unbecomingly ... then you have the right to enslave him.'"[6] In the ranks of "useless persons," were any small landholder who had been ruined, any tradesman who was out of work, or any day worker who was unemployed. The formulation "conducting oneself unbecomingly" gave an even greater opportunity for capriciousness and forced enslavement. It was possible to justify any forced enslavement of the people of the lower strata of the population. These facts attest to the great desire of landholders to acquire slaves and use of slave labor to the greatest extent possible. They seem to contradict the view, offered above, of the gradual disintegration of the slave-owning system, the tendency to free the slaves and to bind them individually to the land. The growth of productive forces, of trade and of the demand for agricultural products and for the production of craftsmen caused the disintegration of the slave-owning system. But these same phenomena led to an increased demand for work hands. The landholders tried to fill the demand for workers by drawing into slavery new human reserves from the free strata of society, the small

---

[1] b. B.M. 64b.
[2] b. B.M. 64b, b. Git. 12a.
[3] b. B.M. 64b, 65a, B.Q. 97a.
[4] b. B.M. 65a.
[5] b. B.M. 73b.
[6] *Ibid.*

landowners, the renters, the sharecroppers, and the day workers. We find praise of work and of the man who lives by his productive labor: "Great is work—it accrues respect to him who does it."[1] "Great is the power of work."[2] "The father is obliged to teach his son his trade."[3] "Not to teach one's son a trade is the same as teaching him to steal."[4] By praising labor and the working man it was hoped to attract into the productive process the largest number of workers.

In enslaving people the large landholders acquired the landholdings of the small holders. The large landholders were not interested in chasing these direct producers from their lands, for this would deprive them of the work force necessary for the newly acquired land. The large landholders preferred to leave the small landholders on their former landplots as slaves. The enslaved small proprietors, who had had their own farms before enslavement, now were turned not into slaves, but into serfs. Thus, the phenomena of enslaving debtors without means, non-payers of the poll-tax, "useless ones" and "those who conducted themselves unbecomingly" not only does not contradict our position on the new relations in productivity created between the slave owners and their slaves, but, on the contrary, to a great degree confirms it. It is precisely the disintegration of the old slave-owning system and the discovery of the inefficiency of this means of production, given the new economic situation, which led to attempts to change radically the approaches to the exploitation of slave labor. This also stimulated the actions of the hereditary gentry and the large landholders of the new type, who aimed at binding to the land by one means or another the whole mass of direct producers. In the final analysis this led to the exchange of the slave-owning means of production for the feudal means.

VIII. Strengthening the Power of the Great Feudal Landholders by Extra-Economic Force

The feudal stratum of landowners was not satisfied with economic means for enslaving and binding direct producers to the lands. They also had at their disposal "extra-economic force." Representatives of the stratum of affluent landholders had administrative-governmental

---

[1] b. Ned. 49b.
[2] b. B.Q. 79b.
[3] b. Qid. 29a.
[4] *Ibid.*

functions. They had the whole legal apparatus in their hands and could subjugate direct producers and decide disputes in their own favor.

Stories about R. Zevid tell of misuse of the administration of justice by landholders. One of his sharecroppers "stole a small measure of barley." He took for his own use a little barley before the harvest was divided between him and R. Zevid. R. Zevid, using his position as teacher of the law and judge, "called him [the sharecropper] a good-for-nothing."[1] That is, the man was not worthy of trust, not allowed to bear legal witness. He was deprived of all civil rights. R. Zevid likewise settled accounts with another of his sharecroppers, who was accursed for only "stealing a branch of unripe dates."[2] The wealthy land-owners, frequently both teachers of the law and judges, could thus deprive sharecroppers of property rights. Taking anything without the landholder's knowledge, even a small bundle of sticks,[3] was looked upon as thievery.

The special interest in jurisprudence which arose in Iraq beginning in the third century can to a significant degree be explained in these terms. We likewise can explain the rise of numerous schools which concentrated principally on contractual law, dealing with landowning, land use, and the like. Taking the administration of justice into their own hands and using it to bind the direct producers to the land, the new strata of the ruling class found it necessary to study the agrarian legal norms existing up to that time, "the customs of the region," in purchase sale arrangements and in renting land. They had to work out new norms to correspond to the new forms of landowning and land use which had arisen, and to relate to the new relations between the proprietors of the land and their actual owners, between the landowners and the direct producers. The feudal landholders tried to influence the direct producers in a way profitable to their own economic interests by ideological means, as well. This is reflected in the rise of new ideas, theories, political views, which corresponded to the new productive relationships, and constituted the ideological superstructure of early feudalism.

It is precisely from this point of view that one should regard the positive relationship of the rich landholders to the new type to labor, the numerous statements of their representatives about the great value of labor, both personally for the laboring man himself, and for society

---

[1] b. Sanh. 26b.
[2] *Ibid.*
[3] b. Ber. 5b, b. Hul. 105a.

as a whole; their extolling the man who lives by the labor of his hands; their proclamation as a religious norm that "the man who enjoys [lives by] his labor is much greater than the man who fears God."[1] But the distintegration of the means of production by slavery, the lessening of interest in work among enslaved renters, caused a sharp drop in the necessary work force. The large landholders were interested especially in the maximal intensiveness of labor on the part of their renters; on this labor depended their income from the land. All of this was the psychological reason, the ideological stimulus, for the rise of such positive attitudes toward work, raising it to the level of religious dogma. This would have been utterly unthinkable under the slave-owning system of production.

---

[1] b. Ber. 8a.

COMMENTARY

JACOB NEUSNER

I.

Solodukho, writing in 1956, correctly claimed that Talmudic literature had yet to be studied from the perspective of economic history. He evidently did not know J. Newman, *Agricultural Life of the Jews in Babylonia, 200-500* (London, 1932), and *Commerical Life of the Jews in Babylonia, 200-500* (London, n.d., mimeographed form). While useful compendia of sayings and stories on various economic matters, these works would not have greatly changed his opinion. On the other hand, F. M. Heichelheim, "Roman Syria," in Tenney Frank, ed., *An Economic Survey of Ancient Rome* (Baltimore, 1938), IV, pp. 121-258, contains important materials on Babylonian Jewry, as on all other economic-historical questions, and Solodukho should have known that basic work. Since 1956 one important study has appeared, Moshe Beer, *Ma'amadam HaKalkali veHaHevrati shel 'Amora'é Bavel* [The Economic and Social Status of the Babylonian Amoraim] (Ramat Gan, 1963, dissertation, in mimeograph form), which, while seriously deficient in historical method, is a work of considerable interest. My *History of the Jews in Babylonia* (Leiden, 1965-1970, I-V) pays only passing attention to economic-historical questions, e.g., IV, pp. 386-391. E. E. Urbach, "The Laws Regarding Slavery As a Source for Social History of the Period of the Second Temple, the Mishnah, and Talmud," *Annual of Jewish Studies* (London) (Jerusalem, 1964, translated from *Ṣiyyon* [*Zion*] 35, 1960) represents the sort of study Solodukho would have found particularly valuable. Urbach makes use of the legal materials for an account of pre-Maccabaean, Maccabaean, Herodaean, Roman, and post-Destruction social history. For Palestine, E.E. Urbach's *Class Status and Leadership in the World of the Palestinian Sages* (*Israel Academy of Sciences and Humanities. Proceedings.* Vol. II, No. 4, Jerusalem 1966) is of similarly fundamental importance. Daniel Sperber, "Costs of Living in Roman Palestine," *Journal of the Economic and Social History of the Orient* 8, 1965, 9, 1966, and 11, 1968, was a major step forward; unfortunately, Sperber's subsequent articles have been fragmentary and noticeably lacking in an understanding of historical method, indeed quite uncritical. Finally, the economic sections of Salo W. Baron, *Social and Religious History of the Jews* (N.Y., 1952), II² and accompanying notes are of some interest for Babylonia, although primarily of bibliographical value.

I find astonishing Solodukho's assertion that a scholarly translation of the Babylonian Talmud into European languages does not exist. While one finds much to criticize, the Soncino Talmud, in thirty-five volumes, under the editorship of I. Epstein, appeared between 1935 and 1948; it was complete long before Solodukho wrote these words, under the title: *The Babylonian Talmud, translated into English, with notes, glossary, and indices, under the editorship of I. Epstein* (London, Soncino Press: *Seder Neẓikin*, Vols. I-VIII, 1935; *Seder Nashim*, Vols. I-VIII, 1937; *Seder Moʿed*, Vols. I-VIII, 1938; *Seder Ṭohoroth*, Vols. I-II, 1948; *Seder Zeraʿim*, Vols. I-II, 1948; *Seder Ḳodashim*, Vols. I-VI, 1948; *Index Volume*, 1952). Inevitably open to correction in numerous places and on the whole subservient to the traditional commentaries, the translation nonetheless is careful, exact, and accurate. Solodukho's translations do not seem to me either significantly to differ from, or materially to improve on, the Soncino version, and his assertion of having made a significant philological advance is in this regard quite groundless. I have the impression that the did not read English. But he did read German, and therefore should have known Lazarus Goldschmidt, *Der babylonische Talmud. Neu übertragen* (Berlin, Jüdischer Verlag: 1929-1936, vols. I-XII), which, I am told, is an excellent translation and thoroughly reliable.

II.

The use of legal sources for social and economic history is a considerably more complex problem than Solodukho evidently realizes.

First, not all laws were equally effectively enforced, and some of them were not enforced at all. So one has to show evidence that a given law actually affected everyday life.

Second, in the case before us, the Mishnah was produced in Palestine. Following Solodukho, we may suppose it pertained to, and reflected the economic-social relationships of, Palestinian Jewry. The Babylonian rabbis may have interpreted the law according to the different conditions they faced, but they accepted the authority of the Mishnah. The legal principles of land-tenure interpreted by Solodukho as evidence of changing social-economic relationships in Babylonia derive, for the most part, from the Mishnah, and *not* from the interpretation and application of the Mishnah to Babylonian conditions. And the Mishnaic law has a history of its own, going back, in one form or other and under one set of auspices or another, for centuries. It therefore seems difficult to accept Solodukho's claim that rabbinic law testifies to the *particular* conditions of third- and fourth-century Babylonia, without isolating those particular elements of legal theory and practice deriving from, or testifying about, third- and fourth-century Babylonia alone.

To take a minor example, sayings about the excellence of labor tell Solodukho that the new exploiting class in Babylonia thereby fostered a social ideal appropriate to its economic interests—and that may well be so. But such sayings are mere commonplaces of the rabbinic tradition, and not of that tradition alone. Shall we interpret the appearance of such sentiments as evidence of the effort of a *new* social class to educate a disciplined work-force capable of supplying necessary labor for feudal agriculture? Then we shall have to conclude that wherever we find praise of hard work, we possibly confront a similar socialeconomic situation. In that case the history of Palestine (among other places) would seem to be the history of the (endless) rise of a new landholding classes of absentee entrepreneurs.

Third, even where Solodukho is on firm ground in claiming a particular law was enforced and does reveal circumstances peculiar to third- and fourth-century Babylonia, one may differently interpret the meaning of that fact. For example, Solodukho is correct in saying that the law of *ḥazaqah*, or squatter's rights, was enforced in the rabbinic courts—and in one way only. He says it was enforced in the favor of those who, through usucaption, would enlarge their existing estates. Thus by seizing a piece of land and making use of it for three years, a man could thereby acquire that land. To Solodukho this means that the powerful landowners could seize the small holdings of private parties. However, all cases in the Babylonian Talmud produce rulings in favor of the original holder of the land and against the squatter (Solodukho's "rich land-grabber"). Further, the original landholder had only to complain in court against the squatter to be assured of his right, thereby nullifying the claim of the squatter. This would seem to me to indicate that rabbinic law and court-action normally favored the original landholder, and not the squatter, and to mean, therefore, the opposite of what Solodukho supposes: the law of *ḥazaqah* favored not the (rich, powerful) squatter but the (poor, weak) landholder. In my understanding, however, the rabbis' indeed favored the original landholder in the application of the law of *ḥazaqah*, precisely because it was only by squatting that *poor* people could obtain any land at all. Further, who would be absent from a property for a period of three years, if not an absentee landholder, engaged in the administration of other properties or in trade and commerce? In making practical rulings against squatters, therefore, the rabbis seem to me to have favored the rich and not the poor. So I find myself in agreement with Solodukho's *general* position, but in detail for reasons quite opposite to his. My criticism, therefore, is that Solodukho has not taken account of a wide range of hermeneutical possibilities in his interpretation of particular laws, and that in specifics he has not established the facticity of his interpretation, either by bringing concrete evidence that what seems reasonable actually was so, or by examining a number of possible interpretations and establishing the priority of the Marxist one.

III.

Another weakness in Solodukho's use of legal sources for social history is his failure to notice striking absences in both the substance and the application of the laws. For example, he does not seem to have paid attention to the use of communal funds by rabbinical authorities for various humanitarian purposes. Such funds were evidently expended on the redemption of captives, that is, of people caught and held for ransom by marauders on the fringes of the settled land or on the caravan routes. But we do not have a single case in which communal funds were invested in paying the head- or land-taxes of people unable to produce the necessary specie. Solodukho rightly emphasizes that such people were sold into slavery to pay the required tax, and that rabbinical authorities approved such sales. But the corollary is that the authorities *did* use community funds for other, not dissimilar purposes. Now who would have gone out with the caravans, if not the class of substantial traders? For them the community funds were available.

Who would benefit from the ransom of people seized on the frontiers or on periodical razzias from the desert? Here the picture is less clearcut. The poor farmer as much as his wealthier employer had an interest in the matter, and one cannot readily claim the employers' need for a secure and stable labor force was a dominant consideration. But the contrast to the use of public money for what clearly favored the commercial classes and to the opposition to use of such money for what clearly would have favored the poorest stratum of society seems telling. Still, what it would indicate, in the ransom of captives taken from the caravans, is bias in favor *not* of the new class of landholders, but of the old, established commercial classes out of which the former supposedly had emerged. What this means for Solodukho's Marxist interpretation I cannot say; it would seem he could assimilate such a fact, since he is able to accomodate far less congenial details into his system.

IV.

Solodukho's fundamental assertion that "the overwhelming majority of people who figure in the Babylonian Gemara represent a new type of landowner" is *not* demonstrated, and I doubt that it is so. It is true that many of the authorities in the Babylonian Gemara are described as men of substance. Some were in trade, e.g., Abba b. Abba, the father of Samuel, traded in silks. Others were heads of schools, who evidently exercised control of substantial resources on that account; it is not clear. But central to Solodukho's theory is the assertion that these were *new* landowners, "who had moved up out of the milieu of craftsmen and tradespeople and had become rich." And this is a statement quite without foundation in sources known to me. The evidence before us simply does not tell us about the origins of the rabbinical authorities. The consequent allegations that the "large feudalizing landholders stood for a new, more progressive means of production" are similarly without foundation in presently available sources. Evidence for such statements would have to include data on the dynamics of economic and social history for the first and second centuries, which we simply do not have, and a great deal more reliable and detailed information on the lives and circumstances of the third- and fourth-century masters, and this too is not abundantly in hand. That does not mean Solodukho is without basis for claiming a tendency of rabbinical authority was to bind to the land tenant farmers and so forth. On the contrary, as E. E. Urbach has shown, rabbinical laws of slavery are much as Solodukho represents them.

The further allegation that the lawyers "undertook a ... study of the legal norms ... to work out new norms which better corresponded to the new forms of land-owning and land-use" is dubious, for, as noted, the laws applied in the Babylonian courts depended upon the already-available Palestinian Mishnah of Judah the Patriarch. Solodukho does not show the rabbinical authorities formulated "new norms", either through reinterpreting the old or through new legislation; indeed, he ignores the question of the relationship between Babylonian rabbinic jurisprudence and the Mishnah. For him all laws under discussion, because they applied to Babylonia, originated in response to the conditions of Babylonia. But this is demonstrably false. The very sources cited by Solodukho stand as commentaries upon, and in close relationship to, Mishnaic law. What would be interesting—and conclusive—would be the isolation of peculiarly Babylonian tendencies in the interpretation and application of existing law. This we do not have from Solodukho. He thus does not "establish the class composition of the compilers of the Babylonian Gemara." At best, he *alleges* his view of rabbinic class structure. But the absence of sufficient evidence over a long period of time makes it impossible to show the rabbis to be a *"new* class of landholders" and the *Gemara's* law to be the deliberate and self-conscious expression of their class-interest.

v.

Further, one cannot say Solodukho has started out without an anterior thesis, an agenda of what he hoped to demonstrate. On the contrary, he repeatedly makes use of prejudicial language, labelling the "villains" of the piece "*landowner* R. So-and-so," underlining the recurrent conclusion that the rich "oppressed" the poor and so forth. Quite apart from the Marxist superstructure, one may discern a rather bourgeois substructure of sympathies—for the poor over the rich, for the weak over the strong, for those free of societal responsibilities over those who bore them. These sympathies, while commendable by themselves, limit Solodukho's range of interpretation and produce a rather one-sided and one-dimensional reading of the legal data. In my view the rabbinical laws and their execution in the rabbinical courts exhibit greater complexity than Solodukho seems willing to recognize. If everything is supposed to show the same thing, namely, that the rich landowner-rabbis ruled the community for their own advantage, then one must dismiss or ignore both evidences to the contrary and complicating factors. One obvious consequence of a monomanic inquiry will be the egregious interpretation in one way only, such as noted above, of sayings and stories either quite neutral about the class-struggle or ambiguous about it. And, concentrating on some areas of law to the exclusion of others, Solodukho entirely bypasses other sorts of stories and sayings which pertain to the issue at hand, e.g., stories about rabbis as wonder-workers, theological sayings, moral dicta, accounts of the execution of public responsibilities and the maintenance of the public interest. I tend to agree with Solodukho's fundamental conclusion and acknowledge his priority in reaching it. But it seems to me the methodological issues are far more difficult and the hermeneutical ones considerably less one-sided than he suggests.

VI.

Solodukho's work requires continuators. That seems to me his single most important contribution. He raises central social-economic questions and presses issues almost entirely ignored before his time and not well investigated afterward. When the study of the economic and social history of Babylonian Jewry and of the implications of that history for the western satrapies of Sasanian Iran and the eastern provinces of the Roman (Byzantine) Empire has progressed to a level of sophistication, Solodukho's work will endure as a major statement. He has the merit of stressing what others had ignored or explained away: that the rabbinical movement, or estate, in Babylonia represented an important economic datum, a social force, a constituent in the class structure—and consequent class struggle—of Babylonia. Alongside their interest for historians of religion, the rabbis of Babylonia must now become a subject of study for social and economic historians. The history of Judaism, shaped as it was by the Babylonian Talmud, will then be illuminated by a whole new range of interesting questions. The way in which the central myths and doctrines of rabbinic Judaism related to the social and economic interests, as well as to the imaginative life, of those who shaped and imparted those myths and doctrines, will have to be explored. No sensible person will suppose that these myths and doctrines will be reduced to expressions of economic and class interest alone, just as none would imagine they will be adequately interpreted only in terms of their psychological substratum. But by stressing the class issues contained in, and expressed by, certain areas of Talmudic law, Solodukho has forced serious and sustained consideration of the social and economic aspect and has thereby greatly enriched the hermeneutical resources of Talmudists, just as by supplying examples of the usefulness of Talmudic data, he has widened the range of facts available to economic historians. After a century of "modern" Talmudic scholarship in which the interpretive framework was wholly theological—and that at a level of banal homiletics—and the economic elements were either ignored or collected, in a childish way, under little rubrics such as "sayings about cows" and "stories about crafts", Solodukho's work marks an important, new beginning.

CHAPTER THREE

THE MAZDAK MOVEMENT AND REBELLION OF THE HEBREW POPULATION OF IRAQ IN THE FIRST HALF OF THE SIXTH CENTURY A.D.

[Translated by Sam Driver, this paper originally appeared in *Vestnik drevnei istorii*, Nos. 3-4, 1940, pp. 131-145]

I

At the end of the fifth and in the first of the sixth century A.D., the Iranian government was shaken by a powerful revolutionary movement called Mazdakite, after its leader—the priest Mazdak, son of Bamdad. Mazdakism was based on the religious and ethical teachings of a certain Zaradusht, son of Khoragan, a native of the Pasa[1] region, who had lived some two hundred years earlier, in the third century.[2] Mazdakism later grew into a social movement among the lower classes of Iran, a movement against the gentry and upper landed aristocracy.

The social principles of Mazdak's teachings amounted basically to the following: all men are created equal; it is therefore a crying injustice if some have greater wealth and more wives than others; inequality in material goods and wives is the main reason for enmity among men; and consequently, it is necessary to destroy this inequality: to take from the rich their goods and numerous wives and to divide what is taken among the poor.[3] Mazdak's idea was immensely popular and attracted a mass of supporters. The Mazdakite movement quickly took on the widest proportions. The Arabian historian Tabari speaks of the movement as a general calamity, the like of which history had never known: "Everyone was in the general misfortune; nothing of the like had ever been heard of before." The reason for the rapid spread of Mazdakism was the sharp contrast between the wealth of the aristocracy and priesthood and the poverty of the masses; the contrast

---

[1] Pasa or Fasa, located in the Eastern part of Iran, in Pars.

[2] *Geschichte der Perser und Araber zur Zeit der Sasaniden. Aus der arabischen Chronik des Tabari übersetzt und mit ausführlichen Erläuterungen und Ergänzungen versehen*, by T. Nöldeke (Leyden, 1879) p. 456; Arthur Christensen, *Le règne du roi Kawadh I et le communisme Mazdakite* (Copenhagen, 1925), p. 99.

[3] Nöldeke, *op. cit.*, p. 141, 99.

became especially extreme during and after the seven-year famine under King Peroz (459-484).

The favorable attitude of King Kavad I (488-531) toward the Mazdak movement in the beginning contributed to its spread. Kavad I even introduced a number of social measures in the spirit of Mazdakism. Kavad's attitude toward Mazdakism was prompted, of course, not by religious motivations or by his sympathy for Mazdak's preachings on the equality of all men, but rather by the desire to use the revolutionary movement among the masses to destroy the power of the higher nobility, which had been trying to limit the king's power for their own advantage. By taking the landholdings of the nobility and destroying their family ties, Kavad intended to deal them a crushing blow and to destroy their power at the root. Simultaneously thanks to Mazdak's teaching, he would get rid of the influence of the priesthood, which was closely connected with the nobility and was its faithful support.

At the beginning of his struggle with the nobility, Mazdak was the weaker. The nobility, in alliance with the Magi, brought down Kavad (496) and raised his brother to the throne. Kavad, however, with the help of the Hephthalites soon managed to regain the throne and establish his rule. On returning to power, Kavad dealt severely with the leaders guilty of dethroning him, and many of the higher nobility paid with their heads. Nevertheless, from that time on, Kavad attempted reconciliation with the nobility and priesthood. This was necessary in order for him to undertake his prolonged wars with Byzantium. With the aristocracy and priesthood unsatisfied at home, Kavad could scarcely have been able to carry on these wars. Kavad's attempt at reconciliation with the nobles and priests defined to a significant degree his own attitude toward the Mazdakite movement after his return to power; there are no data which would indicate that he showed favor to the Mazdakites from that time on.

Later, the constantly growing Mazdakite movement came into collision with Mazdak himself, in part because of the question of heir to the throne. The result of this collision was a bloody reprisal against the Mazdakites, which took place at the end of 528 or the beginning of 529, either under Mazdak himself, or under his son Khusro I Anushirvan (531-579). On his accession to the throne, Khosro led a wholesale destruction of the supporters of Mazdakism.[1]

---

[1] Nöldeke, p. 462.

All these events, obviously, were strongly reflected in Hebrew society in Iraq, where they caused corresponding social and political upheavals. A text, preserved in an ancient Hebrew chronicle (Seder 'Olam Zuṭṭa) of the beginning of the ninth century, speaks of these events. The text, written in Aramaic, tells of the major political events which took place in the Hebrew society of Iraq over more than 20 years, beginning in 508. The events are colored by many additions of a legendary character. This, however, does not prevent us from seeing the basic kernel of the narrative through the patterns of legend, a narrative which contains indubitable historical facts. This narrative is of great value both for the history of Hebrew society in Iraq as well as for the history of Iran and, in part, for the history of the Mazdakite movement.

II.

At the end of the chronicle mentioned above, we find the following detailed text:

> And [the Exilarch] Rav-Kahana died, and after him his brother, R. Huna Mar, became [Exilarch] ... And [Exilarch Huna Mar II] died, and after him Rav Huna ... son of Rav Kahana ... became [Exilarch] ... With him ended the exilarchs from the House of David. And it [happened] thus: the wife of the Exilarch Rav Huna was the daughter of the head of the Academy R. Ḥanina; R. Ḥanina was a great man. A judge of the exilarch was removed and went into the city of the head of the academy, R. Ḥanina, and wanted to give a reading [a lecture on Talmudic law], but the head of the academy [R. Ḥanina] would not let him.
>
> [The judge] went to the exilarch [and told what had happened]. The exilarch sent after the head of the academy, and ordered that he be held all night at the city gates. The next morning he was brought [to the exilarch]. The exilarch gave an order, and they pulled out all the hairs of his [R. Ḥanina's] beard, and he ordered that he [R. Ḥanina] not be given refuge. The head of the academy went, and sat down in the great synagogue and wept; he filled a cup with tears and drank them. Death came to the house of the exilarch, and they all died in one night, only Mar Zutra remained [alive], in his mother's womb.
>
> R. Ḥanina dreamed that he went into a grove of cedars, and took an axe and cut down all the cedars that were in it; there remained [only] one small cedar under the ground; and he raised the axe to cut it down. And an old man came and said to him, "I am David, King of Israel, and this grove is my grove, and what did you need in it? Why did you cut it down?" He dealt him a mighty blow and his [R. Ḥanina's] face turned back.

[R. Ḥanina] awoke and saw that his face was turned back. And he asked the learned men: "Does there remain from the house of David [at least] one man?" And they answered him, "There remains not a single person, except for your daughter, who is with child." He went and stood guard at the door in rain and sun, until the boy was born. And when she gave birth, his face straightened out, and was as it had been before.

He took the child to himself, and taught him, and made him a great man. There was a certain son-in-law in the House of David, and his name was R. Pakhda. When he saw that the House of David had died out, he took money and bribed the king and [the king] made him the head. When Mar Zutra was fifteen, he and the head of the academy went to the king and took the office away from R. Pakhda. And that same R. Pakhda—a fly crawled into his nose, and he swelled up from it so that he died. For this reason, the exilarchs from the House of David have a fly inscribed on their seal.

And Mar Zutra was exilarch for twenty years, and R. Ḥanina, R. Sama and R. Isaac were his sages. In his time, R. Isaac, the head of the academy, was killed.

And on that day Mar Zutra[1] the Great stepped forth—may the memory of our prince [be preserved] in the life of the future world. A pillar of fire appeared to him. And four hundred men stepped forth with him, and they entered into battle with the Persians; he conquered the state and for seven years collected poll taxes. At the end of the seventh year, the *dntq* [*sic*] sinned, those who were with him, and they were caught drinking non-Hebrew wine and they went whoring in the palace of the kings of the Persians. The pillar of fire, which had kept growing before him, disappeared. The Persians took him, killed him—the Exilarch Mar Zutra and head of the Academy—and hanged him on the bridge of Maḥoza. The king ordered that the town of the exilarch be plundered.

And on the day when the Exilarch Mar Zutra was killed, may the name of our prince be blessed, a son was born to him, called Mar Zutra after his father. And [everyone] from the House of David fled. For thirty years, Mar Aḥunai could not show his face,[2] and Mar Ḥiza,[3] brother of the head of the house of Nehilai went and settled in Aram-

---

[1] At this place in the text the words "Mar Zutra" are missing; in their place is a garbled word "mjd," which makes no sense at all here. Historians have tried in various ways to decipher the word as it was in the original text. But all their guesses are fantastic, and their corrections capricious. We feel that the word "mjd" occurred from faulty copying of the abbreviation of the words Mar Zutra: MZ. The Hebrew z is very similar in writing to the letter d and can easily be turned into it. The letter "yod" came from a double apostrophe, which in Hebrew abbreviation was usually placed above and between the last letters [of the abbreviation]. As we shall see below, the copyist of the fragment confused the letters "d" and "z" in another place as well.

[2] To fulfill openly his duties as head of Hebrew society.

[3] One of the leaders of the academy.

Saba. Mar Zutra, son of the exilarch Mar Zutra, moved to Palestine, where he was made head of the scholars. In the year 452 after the destruction of the Temple, and in the year 4280 after the creation of the world,[1] he [Mar Zutra, the son of the exilarch] went into Palestine and become head [of the college of scholars].[2]

III.

The point of departure for determining the time of the events described in the chronicle is a reference in one reliable ancient source, dating from the end of the tenth century, *The Epistle of Sherira*, Gaon of the community of Kairuan. This reference notes that the exilarch Rav Huna died in the year of 819 of the Seleucid era, or 508 A.D.[3] Grätz,[4] and after him Lazarus,[5] and a number of other scholars connect this reference from Sherira Gaon to that same Rav Huna whose conflict with his father-in-law is related in our chronicle. Consequently, the earliest date for all these events is 508. It is true that another historian—Isaac Halevy, the outstanding authority on the chronology of the Talmudic period—connects the reference with another exilarch of that time, the predecessor of Rav Huna, son-in-law of Ḥanina. This Rav Huna died only 10-15 years later, around the year 523. But, in the first place, Halevy's conclusions in support of his hypothesis are quite unconvincing, and in the second place, even if we agree with Halevy's proposition that Sherira Gaon and the chronicle speak of different exilarchs, even then there is no need to move back in time the confrontation between the exilarch and his father-in-law by the whole 10-15 years. This confrontation could have taken place in the very first year the exilarch was raised to his station; this is even more probable. Thus, the question of the time of the first event must be considered fully resolved.

---

[1] = 520 A.D. The Hebrews, like the Syrians, count the destruction of the Temple two years earlier, that is in the year 68 of our system, or 3828 from the Creation.
[2] *Anecdota Oxoniensa. Medieval Jewish Chronicals and Chronological Notes Edited from Printed Books and Manuscripts* by Ad. Neubauer (Oxford, 1895) II, pp. 72, 73. [Editor's note: See also Neusner, *A History of the Jews in Babylonia* (Leiden, 1970), V, pp. 95-105.]
[3] *Iggereth Rab Šerira Gaon* (Mainz, 1873), p. 38.
[4] H. Grätz, *Istoriia evreev, perevod so v orogo memetskogo izdanica* (St. Petersburg, 1883), Vol. 5, p. 326.
[5] F. Lazarus, "Die Häupter der Vertriebenen. Beiträge zu einer Geschichte der Exilsfürsten in Babylonien unter den Arsakiden und Sassaniden" (Frankfurt-am-Main, 1890) *Jahrbücher für jüdische Geschichte und Literatur*, vol. X, p. 122, 124.

It is much more difficult to establish the time of the rebellion of the Hebrew population of Iraq against the Iranian government, and the formation of an independent Hebrew state. The dates in the chronicle are contradictory. The above mentioned reference which states that "Mar Zutra was exilarch for twenty years" does not correspond with the chronicle's claim that the son of the hanged exilarch, Mar Zutra, went to Palestine after the death of his father "in the year 452 after the destruction of the Temple, in 4280 after the Creation" (520 A.D.). The year 520, as the earliest year for all the events recounted by the chronicle, certainly does not correspond with the chronicle. Note that Mar Zutra was born only after the death of his father, the Exilarch Rav Huna. But if this contradiction can be reconciled by relegating the latter reference to those earlier mentioned, legendary embellishments of the chronicler, then in actual fact Mar Zutra was already ten to twelve years old on the day of his father's death. Then also the contradiction between the note on the arrival of Mar Zutra (son of the Exilarch Mar Zutra) in Palestine in 520, and the note on Mar Zutra's twenty years as exilarch is quite obvious. From 508—the year of Rav Huna's death—to 520 is only twelve years in all. During that period, even Pakhda could have been exilarch for a certain time. For Mar Zutra there thus remain not more than 7-8 years, but in no case twenty.

Grätz, nevertheless, considers the date 520 to be the correct one, and draws a chronology on the basis of it for all the events of the narrative at hand, squeezing them all into a Procrustean bed of no more than 12-13 years. The basic contradiction which we indicated above is set aside by Grätz. He says that the chronicle entry ("And Mar Zutra was exilarch for 20 years") relates not to Mar Zutra's tenure as exilarch, but to the length of his life. He limits his time as exilarch to seven years. But since Mar Zutra became exilarch at fifteen, and fifteen plus seven equal twenty-two, Grätz is forced to add to the word "twenty" the word "two."

But in the text, it is clearly stated that "Mar Zutra was exilarch for 20 years." Moreover, one cannot suppose that the fifteen-year-old youth, Mar Zutra, would have raised a rebellion against the King of Iran as soon as he assumed the duties of exilarch, especially since the King had just removed Pakhda at Mar Zutra's request and had confirmed Mar Zutra in that rank. Such a rebellion on the part of Mar Zutra makes sense only after the passage of some years, during which his position was strengthened and his influence in Hebrew society grew. But if Grätz, in his desire to preserve the date 520, handles the remaining text somewhat cavalierly and allows himself to introduce basic changes in it, Isaac Halevy, on the other hand, tries to preserve all the details of the narrative, even the obviously legendary ones.[1] Because of this, and because of the above-mentioned supposition that the father of exilarch Mar Zutra was not the Rav Huna who died in 508, but another Rav Huna who was exilarch 508-523, Halevy moves the time of the rebellion of the Hebrew population of Iraq a whole 40 years forward to 551. Similarly, the time of Mar Zutra's defeat and the fall of his independent Hebrew state is set at 558.

This whole concept, so artfully contrived by Halevy, is necessary to support his supposition concerning the greater length of the period, and it is quite unacceptable. There is hardly a less likely time for such a rebellion: a time at which the Sasanian kingdom reached its fullest flowering, the middle of the reign of one of the most powerful representatives of the Sasanian dynasty, Khusro I Anushirvan. There are no data on any special persecutions of the Hebrews during the reign of Khosro I Anushirvan; consequently, there were no real reasons for the Hebrews to rise against him. On the basis of analysis of the text of the narrative and other considerations, we maintain that the defeat of the exilarch Mar Zutra and the fall of the independent Hebrew state founded by him should be related to the year 529 or 530, that is, to the time right after the slaughter of the Mazdakites by King Kavad, or, with his permission, by his son and future heir, Khusro.

IV.

Bourgeois scholars in Hebrew history have tried to present the rebellion as a movement directed against Mazdakism. Grätz, for example, refers to certain Arab sources which ascribe to the Mazdakite movement an insistence on the communality of women. He states categorically, "In any case, the movement coincides with the reign of Kavad, which recalls to our minds the uncivilized practice of holding women in common, as preached by Mazdak under the protection of Kavad." "The rebellion was organized, in all likelihood, in reaction against a communism [sic] intolerable for Hebrews."[2] "Neither Hebrews nor Christians, clearly, were spared by the Communist epidemic; if only the rich suffered from looting by the Zandiks,

---

[1] I. A. Halevy, Doroth Harišonim III (Presburg, 1897), p. 41, 42.
[2] Grätz, Istoriia evreev, vol. 5, p. 326.

the holding of wives in common was a means of acting on everyone. The purity and holiness of matrimony—virtues always characteristic of the Hebrews—were strengthened by the Talmudic teachings. They could not allow their wives and daughters to be constantly in danger of being shamed, or that the purity of family life should be besmirched. This apparently also moved them to undertake armed resistance to the bold attacks on their family purity."[1] The idea of an anti-Communist, anti-Mazdakite character to the rebellion is supported by the majority of bourgeois scholars in Jewish history: "Mar Zutra formed an organization with the goal of counteracting the introduction of Communism";[2] "This social upheaval affected the Hebrews more than any others. Closely related to it is the rebellion of the Babylonian Hebrews under the leadership of Mar Zutra II."[3] "Mar Zutra took up arms against the Persians and organized a rebellion in order to resist the penetration of Communism."[4] Such are the claims of these scholars.

But almost all contemporary scholars studying the Mazdakite movement, even the bourgeois scholars, entirely reject the idea of the communality of women as ascribed by some Arab sources to the movement. This claim is now recognized as merely an invention of historians inimical to the Mazdakite revolutionary movement. There is no information which would in any way support this charge, made against those who dared attack the institution of private property. Nöldeke says in this regard, "The Arabian historians do not directly affirm that matrimony was set aside by him [Mazdak] as a matter of principle, but the forced taking of wives from those who had too many and the elimination of material and class equality led to it. Any prolonged material equality is thinkable in only terms of holding property in common, i.e., when there is no private property at all. He who wishes to eliminate personal property must eliminate the right of inheritance and the closely connected family. The elimination of the family by the Mazdakites went rather far in some instances, as the Arabian sources testify: 'Soon the child did not know who his father was.' This of course could be an exaggeration, or an unfounded conclusion. But more important is the decision of Khusro I, on his accession to the throne, to reestablish disbanded marriages and to

---

[1] *Ibid.*, p. 10.
[2] *Ibid.*
[3] *Evreiskaia entsyklopediia*, vol. VII: Zutra, Mar II, p. 863.
[4] *Ibid.*, vol. XII, p. 454.

protect children of uncertain origin. But such serious orders of the king presuppose that these misfortunes had mainly to do precisely with the upper classes. As tradition has it, the King of Iran would scarcely have worried about the family and property of the lower classes."[1]

All these deliberations of Nöldeke show how unfounded and groundless are the historians' opinions on the communality of women. The Mazdakite movement was directed toward liberating women, setting them free from the harems. Only the upper aristocracy, as Nöldeke properly notes, could suffer from this, since only they had large harems. Polygamy among the Hebrews at that time existed only to a very limited degree, and then only in the higher levels of society. Thus, if it was only a matter of the purity of family life, the Hebrews would not have had to organize a rebellion against the Iranian government. Moreover, the interpretation of the rebellion as one against the Communist tendencies of the Mazdakite movement disagrees entirely with the chronology of the history of the movement. As noted above, from 498 or 499 onward Kavad ceased supporting Mazdakism; and in the period in which the rebellion must have occurred—the twenties of the sixth century—he was waging a decisive battle with the Mazdakites. Consequently, in no case can opposition to Mazdakism be related to the rebellion against the Iranian government, against Kavad.

It is not by accident that the rebellion coincides in time with the Mazdakite movement, and that it is actually closely connected, interwoven with it—but connected in a way quite different from that imagined by scholars up to the present time. The rebellion was not caused by the opposition of the Hebrews to the Communist direction of the Mazdakite movement. It was a result of internal contradictions in the milieu of the ruling class of the Hebrew population in Iraq and the strong sympathies toward Mazdakism on the part of those Hebrews themselves who were minor peasants, renters, sharecroppers, hired men, tradesmen and finally slaves. The bourgeois historians are wrong in passing over in silence the first part of the narrative—concerning the confrontation between the exilarch Rav Huna and his father-in-law, the head of the Academy, Ḥanina. They consider this part pure legend, undeserving of attention. Actually, as we will show later, the confrontation between Rav Huna and Ḥanina and the following "death in the house of the exilarch" are very distinct links in a chain of events

---

[1] *The Jewish Encyclopedia* XII, p. 706. s.v. Zutra, Mar II.

leading up to the rebellion of the Hebrew population of Iraq against the Iranian government. And only an analysis of both parts of the chronicle's narrative makes it possible to grasp the real current of events and their real social significance. But in order to understand the true social significance of these events, it is first necessary to take a detailed look at the class attitudes in Hebrew society in Iraq at the time and at the character of the relations between the separate levels of the ruling class over a period of almost three hundred years preceding the rebellion of Mar Zutra.

v.

In the second to the fifth centuries, the numerous Hebrew population of Iran lived predominantly in the western province of this state— in Iraq—and was basically concentrated in Lower Mesopotamia and ancient Babylonia, in that area between the rivers where the Euphrates and Tigris come closest together.[1] This region, washed by the wide rivers—the Euphrates on the west and the Tigris on the east—was at that time cut across by many great canals, the important ones stretching across the entire land from one large river to the other. There were also many small rivers, lakes, and ponds. Thanks to this, the region was assured of abundant water for crops and was unusually fertile, despite the rarity of rainfall. But the watering of the land required heavy labor. It was necessary to construct a complex irrigation system: canals and ditches to lead the water from the rivers and lakes to the fields, wells and reservoirs for collecting water; dams and levees along the rivers and canals to protect the fields from flooding during times of high water. It was necessary constantly to see that all these irrigation works were kept in order, to repair and replace them; to dredge the rivers and canals and clean the ditches; to repair the breaks in the dams and levees in time to prevent the fields and gardens from flooding, and so on. Also, much labor had to be expended on bringing water to the field, gardens and orchards from the rivers, canals, and reservoirs. The available land, in view of the high population density, was very limited; every bit of land suitable for farming was used.

At the beginning of the period under discussion large landholdings predominated in Iraq. The land belonged mainly to a few members of the landed gentry, the ranking aristocracy and tax-farmers; their large

---

[1] Nöldeke, *op. cit.*, p. 458, 459.

estates were worked mostly by slaves. From the second century on, new groups of wealthy landowners began to appear; they came from the milieu of merchants, tradespeople and sometimes even the small landholders. Many of these wealthy landowners continued to process the agricultural raw materials and produced cloth, rugs, baskets, beer, wine. At the same time some carried on a wide trade in agricultural products and artifacts of the tradesmen; they also dealt in various goods brought from lands near and far. By the canals and rivers of Iraq, they sent grain, sesame seed, and wines to less fertile areas and to different countries. Thus, for example, the landowner Abba Arika (Rav, d. 247), who owned a large vegetable farm, grew rich from brewing beer. The landowners Ḥisda (217-309) and Papa (IV century) also grew rich from farming; both stated, "If I did not brew beer, I would not be rich." Huna, who in his youth was a small landholder, later became rich from winemaking and trade in wine. Papa traded also in sesame. Huna b. Joshua (d. 410) likewise traded in sesame; he bought goods in places along the banks of the famous *Nehar Malka* (The King's Canal), and transported them on this canal. Abba b. Abba, Samuel's Father, engaged in the silk trade. Profits from trade and produce gave this group of landowners the means to acquire new lands and to expand their properties, which they exploited mostly be renting them out in small parcels to renters or sharecroppers.

VI.

The small landholders usually had extremely small land plots, quite insufficient even to feed the owners. The difficult straits of the small landowners, caused by the small size of their holdings, were made more difficult by the tax burden. The land-tax *(tasqa)* and the poll-tax *(karga)*, which the landholder had to pay, came to one-sixth to one-third of their income.[1] Besides these taxes, there was a number of other duties. The tax burden was increased by the abuses of the tax-farmers and tax-collectors, who extracted greater taxes than required by the fixed government norms. The large and wealthy landowners, in one way or another, could always get around the claims of the civil servants and tax-collectors. The tax burden therefore pressed mostly on the small landholders, destroying them completely. The fields of those who had not paid their taxes were sold by civil servants to

---

[1] [Editor's note: Here Solodukho's reviews the theses of Chapter Two.]

extract the land tax. They were sold also by the tax leasers and by officials of the local government. To make it easier to sell the land of people without means, permission was given to auction off the land without observing the series of formalities usually required for sale by auction.

Complete slavery threatened those who had not paid their taxes. The large and wealthy landowners under Shapur II (309-380) made full use of the government law by which those who could not pay their poll tax became the slaves of the person who paid the tax for them. In order to pay their taxes, to buy seed for sowing, and to feed their families, the small landholders were forced to take loans against their future harvest or to sell their next harvest beforehand at a low price, which contributed to their greater poverty and led finally to their enslavement by the large and wealthy landowners. The small landowner led an impoverished life. The texts say that the small landowner had to feed on salt and grass after the reaping; to sleep on the ground and to have lawsuits with his (stronger) neighbors [b. Yebamot 63a], who tried to take a part of his small plot, deprive him of water rights and so on.

The institution of guaranteeing tax payment, and in part land taxes, also served the large and wealthy landowners as a means of subjugating the small landowners and squeezing them off their land plots. Rich landowners, who accepted for temporary use the plot of a neighbor trying to escape the burden of taxes, would try to pay up the taxes on the plot for several years ahead in order to guarantee his right to the use of this land for a longer time.

The small landowner often had to mortgage his land to pay his taxes and often to get a loan necessary to run his farm or feed his family. Such loans were usually given for a period up to ten years and even greater. During the course of that time, the person who mortgaged his land did not, in many areas, have the right to pay it up. Even when the period for which the loan was taken was not specified earlier, the debtor did not have the right to pay it in full for at least a year. During the whole time agreed upon the money lender had the use of the mortgaged land and received all the income from it. Most often he had the use of the land "without deduction;" the income from the mortgaged land was not counted against the debt. Sometimes it was agreed that the moneylender would use the land free for a certain period of time, and after that, use of the land by the lender would decrease the debt. Mortgaging often led to the complete loss of land by the small landowners; the land would become sole property of the moneylenders. The moneylenders pressured the debtors in all sorts of ways, trying to force them either during the period of the mortgage, or, just after it, to sell them the mortgaged land.

The large and wealthy landholders also used the law of superannuation (ḤZQH) in order to keep for good that land they held temporarily as security from their debtors. According to this law if land or other real property was held by someone for more than three years, the property could be recognized as his own even without exhibiting a deed. Abuses of the law of superannuation by the lenders occurred very often. They would hide the mortgage agreements and say that they had bought the land from the owner. The small landholders also were dependent on the large and wealthy landowners because of the necessity of watering the fields, which in turn involved the use and support of the complex irrigation system, keeping it in order, repairing or renewing it. All this was beyond the powers of the small landholder, and he was thus dependent on his wealthy neighbor; the latter might at any time, on any pretext, deprive him of his water sources. All a rich neighbor had to do was to deepen the canal at some point where it ran through his wide holdings, or by some means block the normal flow of a river or canal, and the fields of his neighbors would be deprived of water—and their owners doomed to hunger. In this way also the large and wealthy landowners forced the small landholders to sell their lands.

Similarly, the law of the "adjacent owner" helped in transferring land into the hands of the large and wealthy landowners. According to this law the adjacent landowner had first refusal on any land bordering his own. In view of the size of the large landowners' estate, any piece of land for sale almost inevitably bordered on them at some point; this very fact decided beforehand the question of who would acquire the land. A Talmudic tale from the fourth century about the small landholder Ronia is a good example of the small landholder's being squeezed off his land by the holdings of his wealthy neighbor. The small landholders found it increasingly more difficult to resist the pressure of powerful neighbors and tax collectors, and to keep their land for themselves. More and more often they were forced to find some other means of earning a living, or else to continue working their former land, not as owners but as renters and sharecroppers, or finally to hire themselves out as day laborers.

VII.

Land rent in the Hebrew population of Iraq in the time under consideration took a number of forms and had correspondingly different names, depending on what was being rented and the manner in which the rent was to be paid. A widespread form of rent was the kind where the amount of the rent did not depend on the size of the harvest, on the income of the renter. If the rent was a certain fixed sum of money, then the use of the land belonging to another was called *sekhirut* (hire). If the rent payment was to be made in the form of a certain amount of produce independent of the size of the harvest, then the renting of the land to another was called *ḥakhirut* (rent). The renter *(ḥōkher)* would pay the rent either in produce from his plot, or in some other kind of agricultural produce, depending on the conditions agreed upon in the contract with the owner. The renter was obliged to pay his rent in full even in years of crop failure, if it occured only on the land rented or the area around it. Only in case of general crop failure was the owner obliged to decrease somewhat the rent payment fixed in the rent contract. But even this disposition concerning lowering the rent in case of crop failure was qualified by so many restrictions that the renter could very rarely make use of it.

A more widespread form of renting land was sharecropping, called *arisut* or *qabblanut*, depending on whether the sharecropper owned fully the means of production or only in part. It also depended on who paid the government taxes, the landowner or the sharecropper. The person receiving land for sharecropping was obliged to give the owner a certain part of the harvest, from 1/3-1/4 up to 2/3-3/4. The sharecropper—*aris*—did not have the means of production or had them only in part, and he lacked the financial means for running the farm: buying seed, etc. The owner rented to such a sharecropper the means of production together with the land. As to seed for sowing, Talmudic literature shows that there were various practices in various regions: in some places, the owner had to give the seed to the sharecropper; in others, the sharecropper had to arrange for seed himself. In actual fact, even where it was the custom for the sharecropper to see to his own seed, the owner provided it, since the sharecropper rarely had the means to buy it. The obligation of the sharecropper to provide the seed meant simply that the seed was charged against his account, and the money spent was added to the sharecropper's debt to the owner. At harvest time the amount spent for seed plus interest on the amount would be added to the landowner's portion of the harvest. Thus the sharecropper was indebted to the landowner from the outset and later fell into complete dependence on him. In a year of poor harvest it was sometimes unprofitable for the sharecropper to bother gathering the harvest, since his portion would scarcely recompense him for the labor of gathering it. The landholder, who did not have to expend any effort in the harvesting, found it profitable to take his portion even from the poorest harvest; therefore, he had the right to force the sharecropper to complete the harvest.

The sharecropper was obliged to deliver the landowner's portion in the form of finished products: the harvest from the fields had to be threshed, winnowed and heaped into a pile of grain; the harvest from the fields turned into wine. The landowner could throw off his rented lands any sharecropper or renter who broke the conditions of the contract or the rules of local custom. Moreover, he could throw him off [the land] even in the middle of the year, thus depriving him of the fruits of many months of hard work and sometimes also of a considerable investment in planting the land. The same fate awaited the renter or landholder whenever it might seem to the landowner that the renter did not take care of the land well enough or did not work it intensively enough.

In this way, new relationships grew up in Iraq at the time under discussion, different from the relationships of the preceding period. Large landowners squeezed out small landowners; the majority of small landowners lost their land and became renters, sharecroppers, or hired workers. The remainder lost the larger part of their land and managed to hold onto an insignificant farm, insufficient for a living. As a result, encumbered with many debts, they became enslaved to the large landowners and completely dependent on them. At the same time, many slaves became directly attached to the land: they were apportioned individual plots with a right to part of the harvest, or on the condition that they give the landowner a certain amount of produce. Renting, sharecropping, and, to a certain extent, hired labor came to replace the disintegrating institution of slavery, as well as the more and more hard-pressed small landholding class. As a result of the sharp social differentiation in the agricultural population and the oppression and merciless exploitation of the workers, the class struggle became acute.

The class struggle was complicated by contradictions among the landowners themselves. The contradictions grew more and more marked between, on the one hand, the landed gentry, the ranking aristocracy and tax leasors, and on the other hand, the newly affluent landholders. While the former represented the outworn means of production by slavery, the latter used for the most part renters, sharecroppers, and hired workers. The new groups of landholders, needing more land, tried to gain access to the hereditary estates of the landed gentry.

The Hebrew population of Iraq enjoyed, over several centuries, a considerable independence; a hereditary exilarch governed the Hebrew population in all the provinces of the Iranian state (as the *Roš golah*, the head of the diaspora, or, in Aramaic, the *Reš galuta*), a kind of viceroy of the Iranian state among the Hebrew population, who had to a certain extent his own special jurisdiction. This is explained not only by the size of the Hebrew population of Iraq, but no less by the role it played in the economic life of the country: in agriculture, artisanry, internal and external trade. It is also explained in part by the special significance of Iraq as a province in the extreme western part of Iran, bordering on the Roman Empire.

The functions of the exilarch were quite broad; he saw to law and order in the villages and towns populated by Hebrews, to the carrying on of trade in the markets, and regulated prices. The exilarch was the supreme judge for all Iranian Hebrews and judged the most important cases at law. For ordinary cases, he appointed special judges for each area and town. He had the right of "the rod and the knout," and could punish most severely those subject to him. He even pronounced death sentences, although he was deprived of this right under the Sasanians. The exilarch represented Hebrew society and its interests before the king and higher government functionaries and gathered taxes from the Hebrew population for the government.

The exilarch lived in extraordinary luxury, was surrounded by a numerous retinue, and had direct access to the King. The income of the exilarch was made up of special collections gathered from the Hebrew communities of Iran. Moreover, the exilarchs and members of their families owned great estates and great numbers of slaves. Being themselves large landowners, the exilarchs represented the landed gentry, the higher ranking aristocracy, and the tax leasors, and depended on them for support. The growing power of the newly emerging, affluent landowners forced the exilarch, from the second century on, to seek support among their own representatives: the heads of the Talmudic schools.

Toward the beginning of the fifth century, the new stratum of landowners took complete power and subjugated the exilarchs. Exilarch ʿUqban and other contemporaries of the head of the Talmudic schools Ashi (332-427) in Mata Meḥassia (near Sura), even had to transfer to Meḥassia, the residence of Ashi, the annual autumn ceremonial receptions of representatives of the Hebrew communities.[1] However, the ranking aristocracy did not lay down its arms, but rather waited for a suitable time to reestablish its power and influence in Hebrew society.

VIII.

The analysis of the social structure of the ruling class in the Hebrew society of Iraq and the relationships among the various strata permits an understanding of the real meaning of the tale from the ancient chronicle cited above. It also allows us to complete the picture of events which occurred in the Hebrew society of Iran in the first half of the sixth century A.D. In connection with the change in attitude of Kavad I, after his return to power in 498-499, toward the higher nobility of Iran, moving toward reconciliation with it, there is also the Hebrew aristocracy which tried to regain its former influence in the Hebrew community. These attempts, which in part took the form of appointments by the exilarchs of functionaries and judges who opposed the interests of the rich landowners, led to the confrontation between the exilarch and the head of the academy, Ḥanina. As a result, the exilarch, Rav Huna, and those close to him were killed. There remained alive only the wife of the exilarch (the daughter of Ḥanina), and her son, Mar Zutra, only a few years old. Ḥanina took his grandson, the son of the exilarch, Rav Huna, into his own house and reared him in the spirit of the social group he represented. After Rav Huna, a certain Pakhda was exilarch for some time, according to further indications in the narrative. This Pakhda was a distant relative of the former exilarch. Then Mar Zutra became exilarch, sympathetic to Ḥanina and the group he represented. The struggle between the old nobility and the emerging new landholding strata nevertheless continued. The Iranian government at this time supported the old nobility. Thus, when in a later confrontation, Isaac, one of the outstanding representatives of the middle landowners, was killed, Mar Zutra had to oppose the government himself.

---

[1] Nöldeke, *op. cit.*, p. 241, note. 1.

The rebellion of the Hebrew population of Iraq against the Iranian government thus took place, because, in the class struggle within the Hebrew society itself, Kavad sided with the old nobility and the large landowners in their struggle against the middle landowners and rich merchants who were growing stronger and stronger. And insofar as the rebellion was directed in its main thrust against the old nobility and large landowners, it was progressive in character.

The claims of bourgeois scholars that the rebellion was directed against the Communistic ideas of the Mazdakite movement are overthrown by the correctly constructed chronology of corresponding historical events. By 522-523, when the rebellion occurred, Kavad's sympathy for the Communistic doctrine of Mazdak had long since evaporated. Consequently, the Hebrews who, according to the historians cited, were struggling exclusively against the Communistic ideas of Mazdak and his doctrine of holding women in common, had no reason to rebel against Kavad. As a matter of fact, Kavad himself was only waiting for the right time and pretext to deliver a crushing blow to the Mazdakite movement, which had become dangerous to the ruling classes. Among the rebels, as it later became clear, there were many rebels who were ardent Mazdakites. This fact is eloquent support for our understanding of the character and meaning of the rebellion.

The chronicle itself indicates that "at the end of seven years, the *dntqy* who were with him sinned," that is, who were with Mar Zutra. The word *dntqy* has never been deciphered. Grätz and other scholars suggest a number of variant interpretations which require, on the one hand a radical change in the word itself, and on the other, bring little clarity to the sense of the sentence. We think it best to change the first letter "d" to "z"—these letters are quite similar in Hebrew script and therefore could easily have been confused by copyists—and the third letter "t" to "d"—these letters are similar in sound, and moreover in the Mandaic language, for example, "d" is assimilated and becomes "t."[1] Then we have the word "*zndki*"—"*zindiki*" or "*zandiki*," which "in Arab literation of the third century of the Hegira (9th century A.D.), besides the general meaning of heretic, often was applied especially to Manichaeans, who were then well known to Arab society."[2] Mazdakites were included under Manichaeans in the understanding of the time.

---
[1] *Iggeret Šerira Gaon*, p. 36.
[2] Th. Nöldeke, *Mandäische Grammatik* (Halle, 1875), pp. 46, 43 and 93, pp. 106-107.

The narrative says: "The *dntq y* who were with him sinned, and they were found drinking non-Hebrew wine, and whoring..." For a chronicler of the 9th century, it is quite natural to think of the Mazdakites as desirous of holding women in common and debauchery. We have every reason to suppose that the "sin" was having relations with Mazdakites who were non-Hebrews. We may also suppose that they were not just satisfied with victory but tried to put the principles of Mazdakism into practice, to divide up the lands of the gentry of rich landholders, and to destroy the existing conditions of renting leading to slavery. This attempt on the part of the Hebrew Mazdakites led, naturally, to an even sharper division between the former allies. When, after seven years of independent existence, the Hebrew state fell, the exilarch and Ḥanina were brought to the town of Maḥoza, which was near the Sasanian residence at Ctesiphon, and were hanged on the town bridge. The town of the exilarch, probably Pumbedita, center of the Hebrew population in Iraq, was sacked.

Significant social changes took place as a result of the Hebrew rebellion under the leadership of Mar Zutra. The main thrust in putting down the rebellion was, without doubt, directed against the Hebrew Mazdakites. The influence of the middle level of rich landowners did not decrease, but rather must have increased. The power of the landed gentry and other strata of large landholders was permanently broken. Throughout the whole of the sixth century and the beginning of the seventh, right up to the Arab conquest of Iran, the power of the exilarchs was insignificant; power now rested in the hands of the middle level of landowners and their representatives.

CHAPTER FOUR

THE PERSIAN ADMINISTRATIVE-LEGAL,
SOCIO-ECONOMIC, AND EVERYDAY LEXICON IN
THE JEWISH-IRAQI LITERARY MONUMENTS OF
THE SASANIAN PERIOD

[This article, which originally appeared in *Drevnii Mir*.
Festschrift for V. V. Struve (Moscow, 1962) was translated by
Sam Driver]

I.

In the course of my work of many years on Hebrew literary-legal monuments of the second to fifth centuries A.D., especially on the broad socio-economic materials contained in them, this question has occurred many times: To what areas and countries can one relate a certain set of conclusions about the character of the social structure of the given period? Should one relate these conclusions only to those countries in which the monuments at hand were created? Should we consider that the Syrian-Palestinian monuments reflect the social-economic structure only of Syria-Palestine? Do the Iraqi monuments reflect only Iraq? Or do they have in a territorial sense a much greater significance? Syria and Palestine were in the second to fifth centuries of our era initially part of the Roman Empire and then of the Byzantine state. Iraq was part of the Persian state. The materials of the Hebrew literary-legal monuments should, consequently, reflect in one or another measure also the social-economic structure of these states as a whole.

The elucidation of this question in regard to the Hebrew-Iraqi monuments is especially important and complex.

In the third to the fifth centuries A.D. Iraq was an integral part of the Persian state. On the eastern border of Iraq the capital of the whole Sasanian state, the city of Ctesiphon, was located on the eastern bank of the Tigris. Thanks to its most fertile soil, its well-constructed and wide-spread irrigation system, its geographical position, good for trade, and to a political situation which had favorably developed, Iraq was economically far better developed than the other parts of the Persian state. The fact that Iraq gave to the King of Persia a third part of all his income[1] is indicative in this regard. Corresponding to the greater degree of development of productive forces and the greater density of population in Iraq was also a much better developed urban life. At that time, when in the internal regions of the Persian state only insignificant cities were found, in Iraq we know, in the period under discussion, of a number of large cities and a close network of middle-sized and small ones.

In view of all this the question arises: to what measure do those comprehensive data about the level of development of the productive powers of Iraq in the third to fifth centuries A.D. relate to the Sasanian state as a whole? Do the processes of change in relation to production in Iraq reflect what was going on in the Persian kingdom? These are data which I have uncovered as a result of careful analysis of the rich materials of the basic Hebrew-Iraqi literary monuments of the Sasanian period—the Babylonian *Gemara*.

The answer to the question, important for the definition of the historical significance of these materials, is given us in my opinion in the first place by the frequent references of the authors of the *Gemara* to Persian legal norms,[2] Persian jurisdiction,[3] to the Persian state dispositions,[4] the rescripts of the Persian king,[5] and so on. In the second place we find frequent indications in the *Gemara* that *reš-galuta* (the exilarch, head of the self-government of the Iraqi Hebrews) judges according to Persian laws;[6] we have the declared disposition by one of the founders of the Babylonian Talmud, the chief judge of the city of Nehardea, the doctor and astronomer Mar Samuel Yarkhina (d. 254): *Dina dimalkhuta dina*[7]—"the law of the state is the law." This indicates that the state dispositions in civil and criminal law were for the Hebrews just as binding legal norms as were the norms of the biblical and Talmudic legislation. They had to be fulfilled not only because of fear of punishment, but because of the recognition of their rightness and legality.

All this undoubtedly follows from the close economic relations established toward the third century A.D. between the Iraqi Hebrews and the population of the other parts of the Persian state. But, on the

---

[1] V. I. Bertol'd, *Irak. Istoricheskii obzor* (Tashkent, 1903), p. 23.
[2] b. B.B. 54a, 55a, 173b.
[3] b. Giṭ. 28b, B.B. 173b.
[4] b. B.M. 28b.
[5] b. B.Q. 113b, B.B. 54b.
[6] b. B.Q. 58b, 59a.
[7] b. Ned. 28b, Giṭ. 10b, B.Q. 113b, B.B. 54b, 55a.

other hand, we also find definite evidence that the social-economic structure of the whole Persian state was in some measure similar to the social structure of Iraq. In this way the facts established by this writer concerning Iraq throw a bright light also on many facets of the social development of the Persian state.

We find in the Babylonian *Gemara* a significant quantity of Persian words and terms both administrative legal, and socio-economic, cultural-practical, and so on. Babylonia (Iraq) "both after its inclusion in the composition of the mighty Achemenid state and later, in the period of the greatest expansion to the west of the Parthians and Sasanians, did not become Iranian-speaking and was not assimilated."[1] Numerous data of the Babylonian *Gemara* eloquently testify that in the period under discussion, in the third to the sixth centuries A.D., eastern Aramaic was the language in use in Iraq. The Persian language did not have much significance. The Hebrew-Iraqi literary-legal monument, the Babylonian *Gemara*, is written in that eastern Aramaic language and not in the language of the Aramaic translations of the Pentateuch and some other biblical books. It is rather in the everyday, conversational language. Consequently, the broad Persian lexicon preserved in the Babylonian *Gemara* also was part of the everyday language in Iraq.

By what shall we explain the penetration of such a significant quantity of Persian terms into the Aramaic language used in Iraq, despite the fact that the Persian population and language were insignificantly distributed in Iraq? The penetration of the administrative-legal lexicon is to be explained by the fact that in political and administrative relations, Iraq was an integral part of the Sasanian state. The penetration of the social, economic, and cultural lexicon undoubtedly indicates not only economic and cultural relations between Iraq and other areas of the Sasanian state. It also suggests that the institutions and ideas themselves signified by this lexicon penetrated into Iraq from other regions of the Sasanian state. These institutions and ideas consequently were typical not only of Iraq but also of the Sasanian state as a whole. They characterized both Iraq and the whole Sasanian state. Consequently the Persian lexicon preserved in the Babylonian *Gemara* has great value both for the definition of the degree of economic and cultural connections between Iraq and the other areas of the Sasanian state, and for the elucidation of various questions of the socio-economic structure of the latter.

[1] A. A. Freiman, "Zadachi iranskoi filologii," *Izvestia Akademii nauk SSSR*, Otd. literaturi i iazyka, 5, 1946, p. 377.

II.

The question of the Persian borrowings in Hebrew-Iraqi literary-legal monuments has its own history, which is more than a thousand years old. During this long period, numerous Talmudic commentators and lexicographers, in various countries—Iraq, Italy, Spain, North Africa, France, Germany, and so on,—who were occupied with the interpretation of the Talmudic text and the explanation of the least understandable Aramaic and loan words from other languages, devoted a great deal of attention to the elucidation of the Persian lexicon, its sources and its semantics. Several monographs are dedicated to this question.[1] Nevertheless many Persian words and terms to the present time remain inexplicable. Many of these words, the Persian origin of which is already firmly established, do not lend themselves to etymological explanation. Researchers and lexicographers differ about both the significance of these words and about Persian prototype they come from.

With the Arab conquest of Iraq in 637 Arabic quickly began to displace Aramaic from everyday use. As early as the middle of the ninth century the Suran Gaon Natronai II Ben Hilai (853-858), began to use Arabic in scientific correspondence. During the time of the Gaon protests appeared against the translation of the Bible, during public meetings, into the already incomprehensible Aramaic language. Arabic was preferred. True, Natronai pronounced the protestors heretics, abandoners of their fathers' faith. But he did not object to the appointment, along with the Aramaic translator, of a translator into Arabic. This suggests the insufficiency of Aramaic translation and the necessity of Arabic.

In the first place the borrowed Persian lexicon was naturally forced out of the everyday Aramaic language. Aramaic was replaced by Arabic. The significance of many Persian words and turns of phrase, met in the Hebrew-Iraqi literary-legal monuments, therefore was completely forgotten. In Iraq itself it was necessary for the Gaons and the heads of the Talmudic academies to explain and interpret these expressions. Persian words were still less understood outside the boundaries of Iraq.

---

[1] H. Reland, *IX dissertatio de persicis vocabulis talmudis*, 1706; O. H. Schorr, *HeḤaluṣ. Wissenschaftliche Abhandlungen über jüdische Geschichte, Literatur, und Altertumskunde*, Frankfurt a/M., 7, 1865, 8, 1869; A. Jellinek, "Sefat Ḥakhamim," *Devarim 'Attiqim* 2, Leipzig, 1846; S. Telegdi, "Essai sur la phonétique des emprunts iraniens en araméen talmudique," *Journal asiatique* 226, 1935, pp. 177-256.

Not comprehending the Persian words and their semantics frequently led the copyists of the Talmudic tracts and other Hebrew-Iraqi monuments to distort their writing, and sometimes even mistakenly to replace, on the basis of purely external sound, certain Persian elements of the monument by other significations, Persian or even Hebrew and Aramaic. Desiring to make the Talmudic text more accessible, the copyists sometimes consciously changed the Persian words for Hebrew and Aramaic ones.

All this explains why in Talmudic manuscripts we find, in considerable quantity, variants of Persian words, in comparison with words in the Talmudic printed texts. We likewise find Persian terms in manuscript copies changed, in the printed edition, for Hebrew or Aramaic words. In the printed texts of the Hebrew literary-legal monuments the Persian loan words sometimes exhibit various variants: one and the same word often is read in different places in different ways. Such variants of Persian loan words in the sources also present themselves in various Talmudic compendia and in medieval commentaries to the Talmud. An especially large quantity of variants and variant readings is found in the monumental Talmudic lexicon of Rabbi Nathan ben Yeḥiel of Rome (1035-1106) known under the name of ʿArukh.[1]

Research into the Persian loan words in the *Gemara* is complex. It sometimes is almost impossible to establish with precision to what Iraqi prototypes, unquestionably of Persian origin, these borrowings go back.

The medieval commentators made use of ancient manuscript copies, which preserved the more correct readings and variants. Nathan ben Yeḥiel of Rome used, in composing his monumental lexicon, more ancient and more reliable manuscripts. These made it possible for him to preserve in his lexicon, in their original reading, numerous Persian words and readings. The printed Talmudic texts either distort or omit them entirely, replacing them with Hebrew or Aramaic words. It is necessary in a majority of cases to give preference to the variants of the ʿArukh over the printed Talmudic text. The author of ʿArukh made extensive use of the interpretations of the Iraqi Gaons and other Iraqi

---

[1] The first edition of ʿArukh, in which there is no mention of either the date or place of publication, evidently goes back to 1477; the best of the early editions was published by Daniel Bomberg, Venice, 1581. In both of these editions are many mistakes, preserved in numerous later editions, in significant degree corrected by Alexander Kohut in his critical edition. In compiling this edition he was guided both by the early editions and by manuscripts: ʿArukh HaShalem, (Vienna-New York, 1878-1892, eight volumes with addendum).

interpreters of the *Gemara* of the ninth and tenth centuries, authorities close to the sources of the *Gemara*.

III.

Not all variants of Persian borrowings and the frequent differences of these readings with the variants of the printed text met in the manuscript copies of the Talmud are exclusively the result of distortions, mistakes, or miscopying on the part of the copyists. Part of the variant readings undoubtedly reflects the variety of dialects and goes back to the time of the composition and the copying of the Talmudic text. Thousands of Talmudists took part in this work. Many of them were not native to Iraq, originated in other parts of the Persian state and also in various regions of the Middle East. These Talmudists introduced into the Persian lexicon borrowed by the *Gemara* dialectical peculiarities of the places from which they came. In the variant readings are attested the phonetic changes of the Persian language and the evolution of its sound system.

True, the basic materials of the Babylonian *Gemara* go back to the third to the fifth centuries A.D. Its composition and editing date from the fifth century, when the phonetic changes characteristic of Middle Persian had already been completed. However, the *Gemara* includes folklore, a part of which goes back to an earlier period, even to the beginning or to the middle of the process of the development of the sounds and phonetic changes in the Persian language. This explains the fact of the frequent presence in the *Gemara* of two or more different phonetic forms of one and the same Persian word. I shall introduce one among numerous examples.

In the *Gemara* 'NR' occurs many times.[1] All the researchers and lexicographers identify 'NR' with the Middle Persian ANAP, "clean, not mixed (wine)." Such a significance appears in two Talmudic excerpts or fragments.[2] In one, 'NR' is opposed to *ḥamra meziga* "mixed wine." In the other the word signifies goblet, drinking cup, another word for a drinking cup**, and also, a measure for liquids in the capacity of one quarter. During its penetration into the Aramaic language, 'NPK' also signified "a pure, unmixed wine." But later the word came to mean "vessels from which one drinks wine," and also "a measure for liquids of approximately the same size."

---

[1] b. Shab. 109b, Giṭ. 69b, Qid. 70a, B.M. 86a, B.B. 58b, Ḥul. 94a.
[2] b. Qid. 70a, Ḥul. 94a.

The word 'NPK' also occurs in the *Gemara* in a different-voiced variant 'NBG'[1] and, with the cutting off of the initial N, 'BG'.[2] These forms correspond to later Persian ones. That 'NPK' and 'NBG' represent one and the same word quite definitely is attested by a Talmudic exerpt, in which it is said that the words written on the gates of Cappadocia: 'NPK', 'NBG', 'NṬL'.[3] They evidently were placed there for general information. All these three measures of liquids are identical and represent various names in various localities. The necessity of such a definition was conditioned by trade in drinks and other liquids.

IV.

In the Babylonian *Gemara* there is preserved a conversation between Rav Yehudah (218-298) and the son-in-law of the exilarch, the supreme court judge, R. Naḥman (d. 320), before whom Rav Yehudah was called for anathematizing an offender who claimed to be a rabbi. In the conversation R. Naḥman used Persian and Greek words. Dissatisfied with Rav Naḥman's manner of conversation, the scrupulous Rav Yehudah, every time R. Naḥman used a borrowed word, would ask, "Really is it worse to speak as it is written in the Torah [in Hebrew] or as the ordinary people speak [in Aramaic]?" At this Rav Yehudah would each time indicate the corresponding Hebrew or Aramaic words. With regard to one of the words used, Yehudah reminded Naḥman of what Mar Samuel had once said: "Anyone who talks like that is [at least] a third vain."

In one of these dialogues between Rav Yehudah and R. Naḥman in both of its forms figures the Persian word mentioned above: 'NPK' and 'NBG'. R. Naḥman said: "Let the gentleman drink 'NBG'." Rav Yehudah did not delay in making his comment according to his habit: "Really is it worse to say 'NPK', as the people say, or 'ISPRGWS', as the learned men say."[4] On first glance the reproach of Rav Yehudah is quite incomprehensible: 'NPK' and 'NBG' represent one and the same Middle Persian word, ANAP, and differ one from the other only phonetically. The reproach of Rav Yehudah can be understood only in the following way: 'NPK' penetrated into Aramaic a long time before the conversation under consideration. It managed to be

---

[1] b. Qid. 70a, B.B. 85b.
[2] b. Ber. 51a.
[3] b. B.B. 58b.
[4] b. Qid. 70a.

"hallowed," in the passage of time, so as to become almost a native Aramaic word. The form 'NBG' had not yet managed to receive the right of citizenship on "Aramaic soil." In the form 'NBG' this word seemed to Rav Yehudah purely Persian. For this reason he considered it to be reprehensible to use it in a conversation in Aramaic in place of 'NPK', which was accepted by the Hebrew population. He therefore reproached Rav Naḥman for the use of borrowed words instead of Hebrew or Aramaic ones.

The conversation between R. Naḥman and Rav Yehudah shows that 'NPK' and 'NBG' represent only different forms of one and the same Persian word. It also gives us precise indications about which of these forms is the more ancient, and approximately about when the phonetic change took place. Rav Yehudah died in 298. Consequently the conversation with R. Naḥman took place in the second half of the third century. It serves to affirm that the sound change in Middle Persian was already completed by that time.

The words 'NPK' and 'NBG' could have in the conversation under discussion the meanings "wine," "pure wine" and "goblet" or "drinking cup," and another word for drinking cup**. In the last instance the remark of R. Naḥman to Rav Yehudah could have the same character as, for example, in Russian: "Drink up a glassful."

Learned men avoid this expression: instead of the word 'NPK' they use to word *'ispargus*,[1] which represents evidently an infusion of wine on asparagus. Such a drink was considered very useful for the heart and eyes.[2] It was recommended according to dietetic ideas to be drunk in the morning on an empty stomach. Evidently it was customarily offered to guests. For this reason the word *'ispargus* became indicative of any kind of drink offered in general, as with the word 'NPK'. And similarly, as the word 'NPK' was understood to mean pure, unmixed wine, so the word *'ispargus* was understood in the same way: *'ispargus* was never drunk mixed.[3]

This is one of two fragments in which 'NPK' can have the meaning of "pure wine." But more careful analysis shows that here also 'NPK' signifies "goblet," "drinking cup"—that from which one drinks wine, rather than the wine itself.

Even in the second of these excerpts, which follows, 'NPK' can have either meaning. Mar Samuel crossed the river on a ferry with his

---

[1] *Ibid.*
[2] b. Ber. 51a.
[3] *Ibid.*

servant. He said to his servant: "Treat the ferry man to 'NPK'.[1] The servant gave the ferry man mixed wine. Samuel became angry at the servant because he had deceived the ferry-man since 'NPK' means "live," that is unmixed.[2] From this some have drawn the conclusion that in the given instance the word 'NPK' is understood to mean unmixed wine. However, we have no proof of this. Even if we supposed that the word 'NPK' was understood to mean goblet or drinking cup, then precisely a goblet or drinking cup with pure wine would have been understood. And when Mar Samuel ordered his servant to treat the ferry man to 'NPK', then the latter expected to receive pure wine, not mixed. For that reason Mar Samuel considered the servant had deceived the ferry man.

S. Telegdi, contrary to the clear sense of the corresponding Talmudic texts and without any proof at all, affirms[3] that in the Hebrew monuments there are two words 'NPK', different in semantics, and having nothing in common between them: "One indicates pure wine, and the other, a measure of liquids." The word 'NPK' indicates drinking cup. But according to Telegdi, it has nothing in common either with one or the other words 'NPK'. The foregoing demonstrates the error of Telegdi's opinion.

v.

In these examples I have shown what an immense significance the comparison of all corresponding texts and their careful analysis has for the correct solution of the question of the semantics of Persian words borrowed in Hebrew literary monuments. Now I wish to show that it is equally necessary to reach a correct definition of the semantics of the Persian borrowings for understanding the Talmudic text, for establishing sense and essence, and for evaluating historical significance.

The Babylonian *Gemara* attests the word ZHRWR'[4] in the following context: "Rabbah [third to fourth centuries] said: 'These three things were communicated to me by the exilarch 'Uqban bar Neḥemia from Samuel: The law of the state is the law. The right of prescription of the Persians is of forty years and these ZHRWRY, who ZBYN the land *le-tasqa* [for land tax]—ZBYNHW ZBYNY."[5]

---

[1] b. Ḥul. 94a.
[2] *Ibid.*
[3] Telegdi, *Essai*, p. 230.
[4] Variants: ZYHRWR', ZY'HRR', ZYR', ZHWR'.
[5] b. B.B. 55a.

The verb ZBYN, which figures in the given excerpt, has, in the *qal* the meaning "to buy," "to acquire," and in the *paʿil* "to sell." In the third person of the perfect the orthographic composition of both is identical. They differ only in their vocalization: in the *qal* the third person of the perfect is read *ẓeban* or *ẓebein*, and in *paʿil*, *ẓabben*. The Talmudic text is printed without any vocalizations at all. For that reason the verb used here ZBYN can be accepted as identical for both *qal* and *paʿil*, independently of the sense of the excerpt. This gave the Talmudic commentators and lexicographers the possibility of understanding and explaining in various ways the sense of the excerpts and the meaning of the word ZHRWR'. ʿArukh translates the word ZHRWR': "a state civil-servant for the gathering of land taxes on orchards and vineyards." Correspondingly, he translates the whole excerpt as follows: "These state civil-servants for the gathering of land taxes, who sold land [of those who had not paid their land taxes on time], their sale is considered to be a sale."[1] It has legal power. Following ʿArukh some contemporary lexicographers and translators also translate in this sense both the word ZHRWR' and the entire excerpt.[2]

The famous Talmudic commentator of the twelfth century, Samuel Ben Meir, explains the sense of the word quite differently.[3] He translates the word ZHRWR': "owner of wide land holdings." The excerpt is thus: "Rich land holders, who buy [from government civil-servants during the collection of land taxes] land [from those who did not pay their land taxes] in order to pay off their land tax—their purchase is indeed a purchase."[4]

The overwhelming majority of contemporary researchers and lexicographers have accepted this interpretation of Samuel Ben Meir.[5] The Persian origin of the word ZHRWR' is recognized by everyone, beginning with the author of ʿArukh and ending with the contemporary Talmudic researchers and lexicographers. However, while in the meaning of "rich land holder" or "owner of wide land holdings" the word is easily explained etymologically, in the sense of "government civil-servant for gathering land taxes" it is difficult to find a

---

[1] ʿArukh 3, p. 275b.
[2] J. Levy, *Wörterbuch über die Talmudim und Midraschim* I, 2 (Berlin and Vienna. 1924), p. 517b; L. Goldschmidt, *Der babylonische Talmud*, Leipzig, 1906, 6, p. 1086.
[3] R. Samuel b. Meir, known as Rashbam, 1085-1174.
[4] Rashbam, *ad loc.*
[5] H. Reland, *IX Dissertatio*, p. 291; J. Perles, *Studien*, p. 122; M. Jastrow, *A Dictionary of the Targumim* etc., I, p. 392a, s.v. ZYHR'.

corresponding explanation. The first half of the word ZHR' or ZYHR' occurs in the *Gemara* in the meaning of "land and appurtinences." In an excerpt of a legal character in which various forms of buying and selling real estate are set forth, it is said: "...if he [the seller] told him [the buyer]: 'all the lands [I am selling you]—[it means that] all the lots which he has [are considered to be sold], except the orchards and vineyards. But if he had said to him: [I am selling you] ZYHR'—then even the orchards and vineyards are considered sold, except for the houses and the slaves or servants."[1] This excerpt definitely shows that by ZHR' (or ZYHR') were meant various land-appurtinences, including orchards and vineyards. The word ZHR' is recognized as identical to the Persian word DZR, which signifies gold, money, riches, wealth, ownership, fields and orchards.

The word ZHRWR' can be thus explained etymologically as being made up of the Persian word RZ and the Persian suffix 'WZR which means "owning." This suits precisely the meaning "owner of wide land appurtinences" or "rich land-owner." The H in ZHR' and ZHRWR' can be inserted as a vowel; it can also be inserted by consonants with the Aramaic word ZHRWR' which means "shining, radiance." This often occurs in the *Gemara*; or by consonants with the Persian words ZHRH—"bile" and HR—"poison." These also frequently figure in the *Gemara* in the form ZYHR' in the meaning of "anger" or "wrath"[2] and "poison."[3]

The correctness of interpreting the word ZHRWR' in the sense of "owner of wide land holdings" is incontestably supported also by the entire sense of the excerpt. All three dispositions given in the excerpt in the name of Mar Samuel are interconnected. The first disposition, being something like the juridical premise for the two remaining ones, says, "The law of the land is the law." Proceeding from this principle, a new one for Hebrew law, Mar Samuel recalls that the 'law of superannuation,' which according to Talmudic law is defined as three years, according to Persian law is forty years. Consequently the Iraqi Hebrews also had to be guided by this lengthened period of the law of superannuation. Further Mar Samuel determined, proceeding from this very legal principle, that the sale for the non-payment of land taxes on land and appurtinences is considered legal. This decision of Mar Samuel is based upon a certain Persian state disposition,

---

[1] b. B.B. 61a.
[2] b. Ber. 51b, Giṭ. 45b.
[3] b. A.Z. 30b, Nid. 55b, Ḥul. 52b.

according to which: "Whoever gives [pays off] his land tax he eats the earth."[1] That is, he may use the fruits of the earth. Consequently, civil servants gathering land taxes did not need the sanction of Mar Samuel. The legality of their actions was according to the direct order of the king and on the basis of generally recognized government law. None had the right to assert any kind of claim whatever for losses caused, or for the loss of the appurtinences of the land.

If Mar Samuel had in mind "land-tax-gatherers" his disposition would make no sense at all. But Mar Samuel in reality had in mind, not the tax-gatherers, but those Hebrews who acquired land *from* the tax-gatherers by paying off the land-taxes of the persons who were not in a position to pay taxes. Before the disposition of Mar Samuel, those who lost their land appurtinences as a consequence of not paying their land taxes had recourse to the judicial courts of the Hebrew self-government, which would require the return to them of their real estate by the buyers. The judicial courts satisfied such requirements, since Hebrew law did not recognize a law according to which land appurtinences could be sold for non-payment of taxes.

This disposition of Mar Samuel was an innovation for Hebrew law. It sanctioned existing general state-law for so-called internal use, introduced it in the form of a Hebrew legislative disposition, and recognized it as a legal norm. Since that time such sales of land, through paying of land taxes, were recognized as having the power of law. Those who suffered would no longer have recourse to the Hebrew judicial courts.

The correctness of this interpretation of the word ZHRWR' and of the whole excerpt is dictated, finally, by the word ZBYN' which signifies "buying," "purchase," but in no case can mean "sale."

Thus, thanks to the correct understanding of the semantics of the word ZHRWR' we find proof that in Iraq towards the end of the second century and the beginning of the third century of our era occurred a process of taking land away from small land holders by the affluent feudal land holders and a concentration of land in the hands of the latter. Since the meaning, "owners of wide land holdings" is indicated here by the Persian word ZHRWR', it is necessary to suppose that in one or another form, an analogical process took place in the remaining parts of the Persian states.

---

[1] b. B.B. 54b.

CHAPTER FIVE

CONCERNING CERTAIN PERSIAN BORROWINGS
IN THE BABYLONIAN *GEMARA*

[Translated by Sam Driver from *Kratkie Soobshcheniia* of the
Institute of the Peoples of Asia, No. 86]

In the Aramaic text of the *Gemara*[1] have been preserved a large quantity of Persian socio-economic words, words from everyday life, administrative-legal words and other such terms. In a study published by this writer,[2] I have already spoken of the complexity of researching them. In the manuscript copies of the *Gemara* which have come down to us, and in the medieval Talmudic lexicons, especially in the monumental lexicon of the eleventh century of Nathan Ben Yehiel of Rome (1035-1106), known under the name of '*Arukh*,[3] we find numerous variant readings distinct from the readings of these words in the printed text of the *Gemara*. In the printed texts of the *Gemara* themselves,[4] the Persian borrowings frequently have various readings in the different texts. It would seem that one and the same word is transcribed in different ways in the Hebrew script. It even happens that the Persian words and terms in the manuscript lists and lexicons are replaced in the printed texts by Aramaic or Hebrew ones. All this complicates the

---

[1] *Gemara* literally means "teaching." Its contents basically are a detailed discussion, interpretation and development of the legislation of the codex Mishnah composed and completed about 200 A.D. in Palestine. The Babylonian *Gemara* (there was a separate Palestinian *Gemara*) was created over the third to fifth centuries A.D. and was completed about the year 500 A.D. in Mesopotamia—Iran (in Hebraic texts of the Middle Ages—"Babylonia"), in the southern regions of which the Jews composed a majority of the population and enjoyed broad self-government. The language of the Babylonian *Gemara* is one of the eastern Aramaic dialects.

[2] Yu. A. Solodukho, "Persian Administrative-Legal, Socio-economic and Everyday Lexicon in Hebrew-Iranian Literary Monuments of the Sasanian Period," *The Ancient World*, Moscow, 1962, pages 344-354, above, pp. 86ff.

[3] The first edition of the '*Arukh* goes back, evidently, to 1478. A Kohut has composed a scholarly-critical edition on the basis of early editions and seven manuscripts, in which to a significant degree he corrected the errors of previous editions: A. Kohut, '*Arukh HaShalem*, I-VIII (Vienna-New York, 1878-1892).

[4] The first printed edition began to be published in Soncino (Italy) in 1483, and the first full edition was published in Venice, 1520-1523.

research of Persian borrowings in the *Gemara* and makes fixing Persian prototypes extremely difficult.

Some of the existing variants can be ascribed to orthographic mistakes of the authors of the lists which served as originals for the compilers of the printed texts of the *Gemara*. The majority have their basis most likely, first of all, in the different dialects of the Persian language both in Iran itself and in neighboring countries; in the second place, in the process of phonetic changes of the Persian language and the evolution of its sound system. This increases greatly the value for Iranian philology of Persian borrowings in the Babylonian *Gemara*.

I.

In the Babylonian *Gemara* we find a conversation between the Persian king, Shapur I (242-271) and the chief judge of the city of Nehardea, a doctor and an astronomer, Mar Samuel Yarkhina (d. 254). Shapur is supposed to have once said to Mar Samuel: "You [Jews] say, [that] the Messiah will come on an ass; I shall send him a superb horse which I have."[1] The answer of Mar Samuel, according to the printed text says: MY 'YT LK BR HYWR GWWNY, "Really do you have a horse which is white in color?" In the lexicon of '*Arukh* the answer of Mar Samuel sounds different: MY 'YT LK K'R HZR GWN', "Really do you have an ass of a thousand colors?" With this in the printed text the answer of Mar Samuel is given in the Aramaic language, except for the Persian word GWWN, *color*; in accordance with the variant of the '*Arukh*, it is composed basically in the Persian way. Beside the word indicated it contains two more Persian words: K'R, ass, and HZ'R, "thousand." It is not necessary to prove, that if in the original text of the *Gemara*, Aramaic words were used, then the author of the '*Arukh*, living in Rome, would not replace them with Persian words. In the original text, consequently, precisely Persian words appeared, which were later kept in the '*Arukh*. But since the copyist no longer understood their significance, he took them to be Aramaic words distorted by one of the previous copyists. Following this supposition, he changed them for Aramaic words, more similar in their orthographic character, considering that, by this, he was re-establishing the original text. Such a supposition was made easier by the fact that the writing of the letters K and B, H and Ḥ, Z and W is quite similar.

---

[1] b. Sanh. 98a.

The authenticity of the variant of the ʿ*Arukh* is confirmed, finally, by the substance of the puzzling conversation. At the same time as according to the variant the conversation is deprived of all sense and carries a naive theological character, in the variant ʿ*Arukh*, it acquires a quite *defined* political significance: Preparing for war with Rome, Shapur I wanted to attract to his side the Palestinian Jews and to assure their support against Rome. Attempts to win Palestinian support were made more than once by Iran and also on the part of Rome and Byzantium. Precisely with such a goal Shapur suggested to Mar Samuel, in an allegorical form, to transmit to the Palestinian Jews the message that he was ready, in case of their uprising against Rome, to give them help in horses and riders. It was not necessary for them to await the coming of the Messiah to free themselves from the Roman yoke. Mar Samuel, in a no less allegorical form, asked Shapur about the amount of the help offered him: Can they be assured that he will send an "ass of a thousand colors" (that is, a significant number of horses), and will he give them essential support in the rising against Rome?[1]

II.

In the Babylonian *Gemara* often is noted the word ṢDR'.[2] The medieval commentator Shelomo Yiṣḥaqi [= Rashi] defines it as a "hempen garment."[3] Approximately the same significance was given to this word by many contemporary Talmudic lexicographers: "A rough hempen material," "a garment of a rough hempen cloth," and so on.[4] The context of many fragments makes it clear that ṢDR' served as an object of wide trade. There were special traders and buyers. One of the legal dispositions of the *Gemara* says: "In sales 'on faith'[5] are counted the payment for the ass, for the driver, for the inn, but not counted is his own labor, for his payment (that is for his own labor) he has already received [from the one from whom he bought these goods]."[6] In explanation of this disposition R. Papa (300-376)

---

[1] O. Schorr, *HeḤaluṣ*, VIII, 1869, p. 110.
[2] b. B.M. 60b—ṢRD'.
[3] b. M.Q. 27b, b. Ket. 8b.
[4] J. Lewy, *Wörterbuch über die Talmudim* (Berlin-Vienna, 1924), pp. 174B, 175A; M. Jastrow, *A Dictionary of Targumim* II, p. 1299.
[5] A sale on faith was called that sale in which the seller informs the buyer just for how much he himself bought the goods, how much other expenses he underwent (for transport, storing, and so on) and how much he wants in profit.
[6] b. B.M. 51b, Tos. B.M. 3:22, 23, p. 278, Is. 2-6.

explains that there he has in mind ṢDRWYY-"Merchants and buyers of ṢDR'," who receive from the person from whom they are buying the goods a discount of four per cent.[1] "Making the goods look better" usually was strongly forbidden by Talmudic law and was looked upon as a deception of the buyer.[2] In relation to the ṢDR', Rabbah (d. 320) made an exception. He allowed the merchants to thin or refine the ṢDR' by means of ironing, so that it would appear finer. In ironing and refining the ṢDR' there was not, in his opinion, any element of deception of the buyer.[3]

According to Talmudic law the buyer could annul a sale if he overpaid one-sixth of the value of the object bought, but only when the seller was a professional merchant. If the seller was disposing of his own personal property, the buyer could not, having discovered that he overpaid, raise the question of pretense, for "things of personal use are valuable to a man, and if it were not at a better price, then he would not sell them."[4] In regard to the ṢDR', however, the buyer had the right to annul the sale even if the seller gave a discount on things of personal use, for the ṢDR' was looked upon as merchant goods even when an unprofessional seller was selling it.[5]

All this bears witness to the broad proportions of mercantile trade in ṢDR'. Along with this the data of the *Gemara* speak about the inexpensiveness of these goods. About this the following excerpt gives eloquent testimony: "In earlier times the burial of the deceased was for the relatives much worse than his death, so that it often happened that the relatives would simply leave him and run away. While Rabban Gamaliel did not scorn fineness of shroud in relation to himself and was buried, according to his will, in linen clothing, even the people after him began to bury in linen clothing. Said R. Papa: 'And now it [burial] is accepted by society even in a ṢDR' at a cost of one *zuz*."[6]

The word ṢDR', in the opinion of Fleisher and other researchers, is the same as the Persian word "cape," "mantle," "blanket or cover," "sheet," "tablecloth," "cover," "winding cloth."[7] The Persian Č is given in the ṢDR' as *ṣade*, which corresponds to the use of the Arabs of

---
[1] *Ibid.*
[2] M. B.M. 4:12.
[3] b. B.M. 60a.
[4] *Ibid.*, 51a.
[5] *Ibid.*
[6] b. M.Q. 27b.
[7] Levy, *Wörterbuch*, IV, p. 210.

transliterating the Persian Č as Ṣ. Such a transcription is usual for eastern Aramaic texts. We find it also in the compound term of the *Gemara* ṢWRB' me-rabbanan "outstanding among scholars," where the Č of the Persian word *čarb* "fat," "solid," "fatty," and in the extended sense of "outstanding," "excellent," is given as Ṣ.[1] However, sometimes, although very rarely, we meet in the Babylonian *Gemara* also the transcription of ṭet (for example, in rendering the word čahar, four,[2] preserved in the form ṬŠR).[3] By just such a method the Persian Č in the word *čarb*, the middle Persian *čarak* "mean," "sly," "cunning" is given as ṬSRK'.[4]

III.

The poll tax in Sasanian Iran was collected individually, from each one separately. Sometimes, however, even the head tax, like the land tax, was collected in a general sum from all the population of a given city or area. But even in this instance the collector prepared in advance lists of the payers of the poll tax, who were obliged afterwards to pay the tax which was laid upon the city or area. In connection with this in the Babylonian *Gemara* the following disposition of R. Ashi (d. 427) has been preserved: "PRDKT helps the city [in the payment of the poll tax], but only when the city has saved him [paying his poll tax for him]. If then 'NDYSK' [saved him by the fact that he was not entered on the list of the tax payers], that is God's help, [and he is not obliged to the city for anything]."[5]

Fleisher[6] considers the word PRDKT a contracted form of the Persian *pardāxtak* (New Persian pardactē) "having completely abandoned worldly affairs," "completely given over to the religious, contemplative life." In interpreting the word 'NDYSK' the medieval commentators of the *Gemara*, and also the contemporary translators and lexicographers as well are at odds. Samuel Ben Meir (twelfth century) interprets it as "a gatherer of taxes," Ḥananel as "an official scribe" "a notary" deriving it from the word DYSK' "document,"

---

[1] W. Bacher, "Ein bisher nicht erkanntes persisches Lehnwort im Babylonischen Talmud," *ZDMG* 67, 1913, pp. 268-270.
[2] b. Giṭ. 86a.
[3] Levy, *Wörterbuch*, II, p. 210.
[4] b. B.Q. 56b, Men. 41a. In the text, TSDK', but Fleischer indicates the necessary correction TSRK'—J. Levy, II, p. 210.
[5] b. B.B. 55a.
[6] Levy, *Wörterbuch*, IV, p. 102.

the Persian *dēsak*. Perles holds to the interpretation of Samuel Ben Meir, but traces the word to the Persian *andāz*—"to count," "to measure," "to define."[1] However, even with the interpretation of Samuel Ben Meir it is quite possible to suggest the origin of the word 'NDYSK' from the Persian dēs—; a tax gatherer could be called an 'NDYSK' because of the document, of the list of the tax payers, which he had in his hands and on the basis of which he gathered taxes.

The etymology of this word seems entirely certain: Middle Persian or Parthian** *andesak* or *andesa* means literally "having relationship to a document"—from the ancient Persian *ham-daisa-ka*. As far as we know in Middle Persian text *andesak*—tax gatherer—is not witnessed. In this case as in a number of others the data of the Babylonian *Gemara* permit us to fill out our information about the administrative terminology of Iran during Parthian** and early Sasanian times.

---

[1] J. Perles, *Etymologische Studien zur Kunde der rabbinischen Sprache und Alterthumer* (Breslau, 1871), p. 107; Levy, *Wörterbuch*, I, p. 105.

COMMENTARY

Jacob Neusner

These comments are limited to historical matters.

Solodukho's chief fault as a historian is his failure to subject the Talmudic stories and sayings to critical inquiry. He takes for granted that whatever we find in the Talmud is, in its present state and with no questions to be asked, a useful historical source, and that the use to which each source may be put is defined by the substance of that source. Thus if a saying is attributed to Samuel, that saying was really said, and said by Samuel. Thus the enigmatic saying attributed to Shapur about giving the Messiah a superb horse is taken as something Shapur really said. Solodukho does not ask where, when, and whether Shapur had studied Judaic eschatology—let alone how he knew Samuel. Forthwith the saying is given political significance, as if no other were possible. Certainly, it is possible to suppose Shapur wanted to win Palestinian Jewish support by promising an ass of a thousand colors. But Shapur's several westward razzias never went near Palestine. He took Antioch, then Caesarea Mazaca, but never Caesarea in Palestine. Nor do we know which war is in mind. If it is the great invasion of 259-260, Samuel had (according to the chronologies used by Solodukho) died six years earlier. Then again, why should Shapur not have sent his message directly to Palestine? It seems to me Solodukho has made things altogether too easy, beginning with the interpretation of the allegory.

The argument that the Babylonian *Gemara* may supply testimonies about the whole of Babylonia, as well as about other developed regions of the Sasanian empire, seems to me dubious. Solodukho finds "frequent references" to Persian legal norms, jurisdiction, state dispositions, rescripts, and the like. But the knowledge of Iranian in the Babylonian *Gemara* seems derivative and unimpressive. It is true that the rabbinical estate took account of those Persian laws to which they were required to conform. These had to do with paying taxes, transfer of real estate, and acceptance of Persian legal documents. But in the very sources alluded to by Solodukho is evidence that important rabbis could not read Pahlavi, though they could understand it when it was read to them. Such evidence points to the opposite of Solodukho's conclusion.

As suggested in this writer's *History of the Jews in Babylonia*, the Babylonian Jews were an unimportant minority in the western satrapies of Iran; the rabbis knew about as much Pahlavi as they had to know; they exhibit little knowledge of, or insight into, Iranian cultural, religious, and political affairs, other than those few obvious facts that impinged upon the consciousness of a minority community. They did not even know about all the Iranian religious festivals, but only about those on which taxes had to be paid. The exilarch in this regard may have differed, but he did not "judge according to Persian laws" except as required. Samuel's famous saying that the law of the state is law indicates far less than what Solodukho claims, when one examines the cases to which that saying is applied. They concern, as stated, paying taxes and transferring real estate, not much else. And it certainly is a vast overstatement to claim Samuel thereby recognized the "rightness and legality" of Persian law. What he seems to me to have recognized was simply the requirements of the Jews' subordinated situation.

As to the Jews' language, it was *an* eastern Aramaic, but not the *same* eastern Aramaic as that used by Mandaeans and Christians.

To be sure, Babylonia was an integral part of the Sasanian state. But that does not justify the claim that what we know about Babylonia is routinely to be applied elsewhere. And the evidences of the Babylonian *Gemara* cannot be freely applied to other religious minorities besides the Jews, or in particular, those Jews who are represented by the rabbinical sources—certainly not even the whole of the Jewish population.

INDEX OF TALMUDIC PASSAGES[1]

BABYLONIAN TALMUD

'Avodah Zarah
30b	96n

Bava Batra
12a	24n
25a	49n, 50n
29a	28n
30a-b	21n
32a-b	21n
33b	21n
38a	27n, 28n
40b	21n, 28n
41a	14n
45b	25n
54a	19n, 87n
54b	21n, 87n, 97n
55a	25n, 87n, 94n, 102n
58b	91n, 92n
61a	96n
90b	19n
91a	14n, 16n
168b	21n
173b	87n

Bava Meṣi'a'
10a	46n
15a	46n
33b	15n
27a	48n
28b	87n
51a	101n
51b	100n
60a	101n
60b	100n
64b	48n, 55n
65a	55n
66b	14n
67b	16n, 27n
68a	26n, 27n
69a	33n
69b	40n
72b	16n
73a	37n, 44n

73a-b	26n
73b	53n, 55n
74b	32n, 40n
76a	44n, 45n
76b	44n, 47n
77a	44n, 45n, 46n
83a	44n, 47n
86a	91n
86b	45n
89b	44n
91b	45n
93a	44n
96a	53n
103b	30n, 32n, 39n
104a	39n
104b	36n, 40n
105a	30n, 32n
105b	39n
106a	30n
106	14n, 39n
107b	14n, 20n
108a	20n
108b	25n
108a-b	21n, 22n
109a	42n, 43n
109b	26n, 31n, 41n
110a	31n, 35n
110b	43n
118a	24n

Bava Qamma
27b	14n
56b	102n
58b	87n
59a	87n
79b	21n, 56n
80a	21n
92a	34n
97a	48n, 55n
112b	48n
113a	25n
113b	32n, 87n
116b	46n, 47n
117b	20n

Berakhot
5a	19n, 34n
5b	20n, 57n
8a	58n
16a	45n
17b	44n
31a	18n
34	49n
46a	45n
47b	49n
51a	92n, 93n
51b	18n, 96n
58a	14n

'Eruvin
21a	14n
59a	18n
64a	43n
72b	49n
73a	49n, 50n
100a,	14n

Giṭṭin
10b	25n, 87n
12a	51n, 52n, 55n
28b	87n
38b	48n, 49n
40a	47n
45b	96n
60b	14n, 15n
65b	19n
69b	91n
73a	20n
74b	31n, 38n
74b	31n, 38n
86a	102n

Ḥullin
52b	96n
94a	91n, 94n
105a	14n, 34n, 57n

Ketuvot
8b	100n

[1] Indices were prepared by Mr. Arthur Woodman, Canaan, New Hampshire, on a grant from Brown University.

INDEX OF TALMUDIC PASSAGES

54a	43n	55a	18n	98a	99n
91b	23n	55b	96n		
105a	15n, 19n			Shabbat	
		Pesaḥim		109b	91n
Megillah		107a	19n		
28a	19n			Shevu'ot	
		Qiddushin		46b	43n
Mo'ed Qaṭan		20a	54n		
12b	19n	29a	56n	Ta'anit	
27b	100n, 101n	33a	19n	10a	14n
		49b	48n	19b	49n
Menaḥot		70a	91n, 92n, 93n	25b	49n, 50n
41a	102n	70b	49n		
				Yevamot	
Nedarim		Sanhedrin		46a	54n
28a	25n	7a	14n	63a	21n, 23n, 78
28b	87n	25b	25n		
46b	15n	26b	33n, 57n	Yoma	
49b	56n	58b	23n	75b	33n

MISHNAH

Bava Meṣi'a'		9:8	30n	7:7	21n
4:12	101n	9:9	30n		
5:8-9	40n			Demai	
9:3	39n	Bava Qamma		11:5	21n

TOSEFTA

Bava Meṣi'a'		9:31	30n	Pe'ah	
3:22	100n			3:1	44n
9:2	33n	Demai			
9:19	32n	6:15-16	29n		

PALESTINIAN TALMUD

Bava Meṣi'a'		Ta'anit		
6:1	44n	1:1	50n	

GENERAL INDEX

Abba bar Abba, 18-20, 24, 34, 63, 77
Abba Arika, 11, 19-21, 47, 77
Abbayye, 11, 15, 34-35
Abina, 19
Ada, 49
Addu, 13
Administrative law, 86-97
Aḥa of Difti, R., 36
Alexander of Macedon, 16
Anileus, 2
Animal husbandry, 20-21, 53
Antioch, 104
Aram-Saba, 70
Ardashir of Mesene, 17
Ashi, R., 11, 26, 36, 83, 102
Asinei, 2

Bamdad, 67
Baron, Salo W., 60
Bartol'd, V. V., 16n
Batti bar Tuvyah, 49
Beer, G., 50n
Beer, Moshe, 59
Bé Miksé, 54
Betterment, charges for, 41-43
Bomberg, Daniel, 90n

Caesarea Mazaca, 104
Canaan, 3-4
Cappadocia, 92
Captives, redemption of, 62
China trade, 16
Christensen, Arthur, 67n
Class struggle, viii, 64; landowners as lawgivers, 10-58, 63-64; slaves, 4-7
Communal funds, 62-63
Community property, 67-85
Contractural relationships, 10-11, 57
Corporal punishment, 6-7
Crafts, 3; hereditaments and feudalism, 17-23; Iraq, 15-17; slaves in, 7-8
Criminal law, 10-11
Crop controls, 29-43
Ctesiphon, 85-86

Daskarta estates, 47
Day workers, 43-47

Economic history and structure, 63-66, 86-97; feudal landholders, 56-58; Iraq, 10-58; laws of Talmud, vii
Ejection from land, 38
Eleazar, R., 23
Engels, Friedrich, 3, 17n, 48n
Entrepreneurship, viii
Epstein, I., 60
Ethiopia, 3-4
Export of slaves, 7-8

Factors and tenant farmers, 45
Family, slaves and civil rights, 5-6; social structure, 10-11
Feudalism, 4-9, 17-23
Food services, 45
Frank, Tenny, 59
Freiman, A. A., 88n

Gemara, Persian borrowings, 97-103
Geniva, 19
Gentiles, loans from, 54
Germanic tribes, 3-4
Goldschmidt, Lazarus, 60, 95n
Grätz, H., 71-72, 73n, 84

Halevy, Isaac, 71, 73
Ḥananel, R., 102
Ḥanina, R., 69-71, 75, 83, 85
Heichelheim, F. M., 59
Hephthalites, 68
Ḥisda, R., 11, 19, 34, 38, 77
Ḥiyya b. Joseph, R., 47
Hoshaya Rabba, R., 14
Huna, R., 11, 14, 20, 34
Huna b. Ḥiyya, R., 18-19
Huna bar Jacob, 11
Huna b. Joseph, 77
Huna ben Joshua, 20
Huna Mar, R., 69
Huna Mar II, 69

Ilish, R., 53
Improvements, charges for, 41-43
India, 16
Irrigation, economic pressures from, 2-3, 14-15, 17, 28-44

GENERAL INDEX 109

Isaac, R., 70, 83

Jastrow, M., 95n, 100n
Jellinek, A., 89n
Jonathan, 49
Joseph, R., 24, 32
Josephus Flavius, 4
Joseph, R., 42-43, 50, 55
Joseph b. Ḥiyya, R., 11
Judah bar Papa, R., 49
Judah ben Bathyra, R., 20

Kahana, R., 36
Kairuan, 71
Kavad I, 68, 73, 75, 83-84
Khotagan, 67
Khusro I Anushirvan, 68, 73-75
King's Canal, 20, 77
Kohut, Alexander, 90n, 98

Land, abutters rights of purchase, 21-23, aristocracy of owners, 2-3; grabbers, 61-62; owners as lawgivers, 10-58, 63-64; purchases, 21-23; rabbis owning, 64-65; rents, 2-3, 29-43, 80-83; slavery, Mazdak rebellion, 76-79; taxes and serfdom 2-3, 23-29, 32, 62, 77-83 use, 13-17, 36-43
Lazarus, F., 71
Lease-holds, 11
Levy, J., 50n, 95n, 100n, 101n, 102n, 103n
Liability, animals and workers, 53

Maḥoza, 49, 53
Mar, 37
Mar Aḥunai, 70
Mar Ḥiza, 70
Mari, 35
Maritime trade, 8
Marriage, slaves and civil rights, 5-6
Mar Samuel, 18-19, 34, 49, 92, 96-97
Mar Samuel Yarkhinai, 11, 87, 99-100
Marti, K., 50n
Marx, Karl, vii-ix 17, 48n
Mar Zuttra, 2, 69-72, 76, 83-85
Mar Zuttra II, 74
Mata Meḥasia, 26, 83
Mazdakite rebellion, viii, 67-85
Messiah, 104; and Shapur I, 99-100
Moneylenders, 4, 22-29, 54
Mortgage land, 27

Naḥman, R., 18, 33, 35, 48, 55, 92-94
Naḥman b. Jacob, R., 11
Naresh, 27
Nathan ben Yeḥiel, R., 90, 98
Natronai II Ben Hilai, 89
Nehardea, 19, 40, 87, 99
Nehar Malka (King's Canal), 20, 77
Neubauer, Ad., 71n
Newman, J., 59
Nisibis, 20
Nitzoi, 18
Nöldeke, T., 67n, 74-75, 76n, 83n, 84n

Pakhda, R., 70, 72, 83
Papa, R., 11, 19, 21, 53-54, 77, 100-101
Papa bar Abba, 54
Perles, J., 95n
Peroz, King, 68
Poll taxes, 2-3, 53-54, 56, 62, 102-103;
  Mazdak rebellion, 77-83
Property, slaves rights to, 5-6
Pumbedita, 49, 85

Raba bar bar Hana, 47
Rabbah, 11, 55, 101
Rabban Gamaliel, 101
Rabina, 36, 42
Rashi, 100
Rav, 14, 19-21, 47, 77
Rava, 18-19, 24, 33, 37, 42, 46, 48-49, 53-55
Rav Huna, 71-73, 75, 83
Rav Judah, 13, 35, 42-43, 49, 92-4
Rav-Kahana, 69
Rebellion, 7, 67-85
Reland, H., 89n, 95n
Rent agreements, 29-43
Ronia, 42, 79

Sabbath law, 7-8
Saffron, 14
Sama, R., 70
Samuel, 34-35, 104
Samuel Ben Meir, 95, 102-103
Se'oram, 55
Serfdom, 29-43
Shapur I, 104; and Messiah, 99-100
Shapur II, 9, 53, 78
Sharecroppers, feudalism, 11, 19, 23-43; Mazdak rebellion, 80-83; productivity, 8-9; taxes resulting in, 2-3

Sherira, R., 71
Shelomo Yiṣḥaqi, 100
Sheshet, R., 53
Shimi ben Ashi, 15
Slavery, viii, 63; acquiring slaves, 3-4; areas of use, 7-8; chattel property, 4-7; corporal punishment, 6-7; crafts, 7-8; economic influence, 1-9; exploitation, 47-56; exportation, 7-8; hereditaments and feudalism, 17-23; land taxes and takings, 23-29; landowner as lawgiver, 10-58; legal and social position, 4-7; liability for, 6-7; maritime trade, 8; marriage, 5-6; Mazdak rebellion, 76-83; political influences, 1-9; progeny of slaves, civil rights, 5-6; property, conditional ownership, 5-6; rebellion, 7, 76-83; signs of servitude, 6-7; trade curtailing slavery, 48-56; trades and crafts, 7-8
Social history and structure, 1-58, 63-66, 86-97
Sperber, Daniel, 59
Squatters, 61

Straw, control over, 32
Sura academy, 11, 27

Tabari, 67
Tatoos and slaves, 6-7
Taxes, 62; land takings, 23-29, 32; Mazdak rebellion, 77-83; slavery slavery resulting from, 2-3
Telegdi, S., 89n, 94
Tenant farmers, 11, 14; serfdom, 29-43
Theft enslaving offender, 4, 33
Trades and crafts, 15-17; class structure 3, 47; curtailing slave system, 48-56; Persian influences, 100-102; slaves, use of, 7-8

'Uqban, 83
'Uqban bar Nehemia, 94
Urbach, E. E., 59, 63

Wives, Mazdakites, 67-85
Workers and day workers, 43-47

Zaradusht, 67
Zevid, R., 33, 57

www.ingramcontent.com/pod-product-compliance
Lightning Source LLC
Chambersburg PA
CBHW071455160426
43195CB00013B/2112